INTRODUCING
ISSUES WITH
OPPOSING
VIEWPOINTS®

Abortion

Emma Carlson Berne, *Book Editor*

Christine Nasso, *Publisher*
Elizabeth Des Chenes, *Managing Editor*

GREENHAVEN PRESS
An imprint of Thomson Gale, a part of The Thomson Corporation

THOMSON

GALE

Detroit • New York • San Francisco • New Haven, Conn • Waterville, Maine • London

THOMSON

‐‐‐‐‐‐★‐‐‐‐‐‐ ™

GALE

© 2007 Thomson Gale, a part of The Thomson Corporation.

Thomson and Star Logo are trademarks and Gale and Greenhaven Press are registered trademarks used herein under license.

For more information, contact
Greenhaven Press
27500 Drake Rd.
Farmington Hills, MI 48331-3535
Or you can visit our Internet site at http://www.gale.com

LIBRARY OF CONGRESS CATALOGING-IN-PUBLICATION DATA

Abortion / Berne, Emma Carlson, book editor.
  p. cm. -- (Introducing issues with opposing viewpoints)
  Includes bibliographical references and index.
  ISBN-13: 978-0-7377-3563-5 (hardcover)
  1. Abortion--United States. 2. Abortion--Moral and ethical aspects. I. Carlson Berne,
  Emma.
HQ767.5.U5A2255 2007
363.460973—dc22   2007003663

ISBN-10: 0-7377-3563-5

Printed in the United States of America

Contents

Foreword

I ndulging in a wide spectrum of ideas, beliefs, and perspectives is a critical cornerstone of democracy. After all, it is often debates over differences of opinion, such as whether to legalize abortion, how to treat prisoners, or when to enact the death penalty, that shape our society and drive it forward. Such diversity of thought is frequently regarded as the hallmark of a healthy and civilized culture. As the Reverend Clifford Schutjer of the First Congregational Church in Mansfield, Ohio, declared in a 2001 sermon, "Surrounding oneself with only like-minded people, restricting what we listen to or read only to what we find agreeable is irresponsible. Refusing to entertain doubts once we make up our minds is a subtle but deadly form of arrogance." With this advice in mind, Introducing Issues with Opposing Viewpoints books aim to open readers' minds to the critically divergent views that comprise our world's most important debates.

Introducing Issues with Opposing Viewpoints simplifies for students the enormous and often overwhelming mass of material now available via print and electronic media. Collected in every volume is an array of opinions that captures the essence of a particular controversy or topic. Introducing Issues with Opposing Viewpoints books embody the spirit of nineteenth-century journalist Charles A. Dana's axiom: "Fight for your opinions, but do not believe that they contain the whole truth, or the only truth." Absorbing such contrasting opinions teaches students to analyze the strength of an argument and compare it to its opposition. From this process readers can inform and strengthen their own opinions, or be exposed to new information that will change their minds. Introducing Issues with Opposing Viewpoints is a mosaic of different voices. The authors are statesmen, pundits, academics, journalists, corporations, and ordinary people who have felt compelled to share their experiences and ideas in a public forum. Their words have been collected from newspapers, journals, books, speeches, interviews, and the Internet, the fastest growing body of opinionated material in the world.

Introducing Issues with Opposing Viewpoints shares many of the well-known features of its critically acclaimed parent series, Opposing Viewpoints. The articles are presented in a pro/con format, allowing readers to absorb divergent perspectives side by side. Active reading questions preface each viewpoint, requiring the student to approach the material thoughtfully and carefully. Useful charts, graphs, and cartoons supplement each article. A thorough introduction provides readers with crucial background on an issue. An annotated bibliography points the reader toward articles, books, and Web sites that contain additional information on the topic. An appendix of organizations to contact contains a wide variety of charities, nonprofit organizations, political groups, and private enterprises that each hold a position on the issue at hand. Finally, a comprehensive index allows readers to locate content quickly and efficiently.

Introducing Issues with Opposing Viewpoints is also significantly different from Opposing Viewpoints. As the series title implies, its presentation will help introduce students to the concept of opposing viewpoints, and learn to use this material to aid in critical writing and debate. The series' four-color, accessible format makes the books attractive and inviting to readers of all levels. In addition, each viewpoint has been carefully edited to maximize a reader's understanding of the content. Short but thorough viewpoints capture the essence of an argument. A substantial, thought-provoking essay question placed at the end of each viewpoint asks the student to further investigate the issues raised in the viewpoint, compare and contrast two authors' arguments, or consider how one might go about forming an opinion on the topic at hand. Each viewpoint contains sidebars that include at-a-glance information and handy statistics. A Facts About section located in the back of the book further supplies students with relevant facts and figures.

Following in the tradition of the Opposing Viewpoints series, Greenhaven Press continues to provide readers with invaluable exposure to the controversial issues that shape our world. As John Stuart Mill once wrote: "The only way in which a human being can make some approach to knowing the whole of a subject is by hearing what can be said about it by persons of every variety of opinion and studying all modes in which it can be looked at by every character of mind. No wise man ever acquired his wisdom in any mode but this." It is to this principle that Introducing Issues with Opposing Viewpoints books are dedicated.

Introduction

"It is a moral necessity that we not be forced to bring children into the world for whom we cannot be responsible and adoring and present. We must not inflict life on children who will be resented; we must not inflict unwanted children on society."

—Anne Lamott, novelist and essayist

Not since civil rights has there been a topic as emotional and controversial for American society as abortion. Whether the procedure should be legal or illegal is debated in virtually every format available: on the Internet, on television, in the newspapers, on the floors of Congress, on the streets. People wear buttons, carry placards, and paste bumper stickers on their cars that state where they stand on the topic.

The length and intensity of the debate testifies to the complexity of the issue. Abortion falls into a gray area of society's rights and wrongs. At the heart of the matter is the question, what is a fetus? Some groups, including women's rights organizations and some health-care providers such as Planned Parenthood, believe that a fetus is a part of a woman's body. It is dependent on her for life, and thus it is her own. Others believe that a fetus is a separate human being, apart from the mother. These groups include some conservative political organizations and religious bodies such as the Catholic Church.

Depending on the definition of a fetus, different laws apply to abortion. If a fetus is part of a woman, laws that protect privacy and individual autonomy give the pregnant woman the right to do what she wishes with her body, including her fetus. These are the same laws that permit people to pierce their ears, for instance, or dye their hair. American society as a rule does not invade the personal privacy of its citizens.

The situation is quite different if a fetus is defined as a separate human being. If this is the case, the laws that forbid harming or killing other people apply. These are some of society's deepest-rooted mores. No person may bring harm to another person—including babies. If a fetus is a separate human, it is protected under these laws.

In order to answer the central question, what is a fetus?, many have asked another question: When does a fetus's life begin? There are myriad answers. Some state that a fetus's life begins at the moment of conception. Others say that it begins when the fertilized egg implants in the womb. Still others believe it begins when the fetus develops a heartbeat and a nervous system, or when it can live separately from the pregnant woman, or at the moment of birth. People tend to divide themselves into abortion supporters or opponents based on when they believe a fetus's life begins.

Pro-choice supporters have typically been women's rights groups such as the National Organization for Women (NOW), reproductive rights organizations such as NARAL Pro-Choice America, and socially liberal political groups. These groups have long agitated for legal, available abortion, stating that women's bodies are their own to do with what they wish. Moreover, a fetus is *not* the same as an infant child. It is a part of the pregnant woman. The issue is compli-

A positive pregnancy test is the first step in a woman's journey through the abortion decision-making process.

cated, though, as Lynn Paltrow, the executive director of National Advocates for Pregnant Women, writes: "To oppose the recognition of fetal personhood as a matter of law is not to deny the value of potential life as a matter of religious belief, emotional conviction or personal experience. Rather, it is to recognize that such a legal construct effectively removes pregnant women from the protections of the Constitution and civil law." By recognizing a fetus as a person, these groups argue, a woman loses control over her body.

The pro-life movement disagrees strongly with this reasoning. This group is diverse but includes socially conservative organizations such as Concerned Women for America and the Heritage Foundation, as well as religious entities such as the Catholic Church and some Protestant churches. Pro-life supporters believe that aborting a fetus is akin to murder. As Mark H. Creech, a Protestant minister, writes in the religious publication the *Christian Post*: "[Over] 44 million precious lives have been destroyed since abortion was legalized in the U.S. . . . Fears regarding unplanned pregnancies have obviously created a holocaust unprecedented in human history." Women may carry the fetus, but they do not have rights over it, pro-life groups contend. The fetus belongs to society and is protected under the societal laws that prohibit harm to another.

In 1973 the Supreme Court of the United States ruled on the issue in the famous and controversial *Roe v. Wade* decision. In the majority opinion, Justice Harry Blackmun wrote that in the early stages of pregnancy, when the fetus could not live outside of the mother's body, she had a "right to privacy." This included the right to an abortion. During the later states of pregnancy, when the fetus could conceivably live without the mother, abortion could be prohibited.

Abortion is technically legal, but that has not quieted the debate. Dozens of other issues have arisen. For instance, some have argued that it is not ethical for a woman to abort a fetus that has birth defects. Others have focused on whether or not fetuses in utero can feel pain and whether or not that should make a difference. Some state legislatures have passed laws banning abortion or certain types of abortion procedures in an effort to bring the issue back to the courts. South Dakota took the most extreme step in 2006 when it proposed a bill that would ban all abortions. The proposal was defeated, however, in the 2006 midterm elections.

Many people would like to see *Roe* overturned. Others have worked fiercely to uphold it. Both sides believe they are defending sacred principles: the right of an individual to her own body and the right of a person to be protected from harm. The issue is complex and highly emotional. *Introducing Issues with Opposing Viewpoints: Abortion* will identify and discuss key aspects of this important debate.

Chapter 1

Is Abortion Ethical?

The ethical implications of abortion are the subject of much debate and protest.

Abortion Is Not Ethical

Eugene F. Diamond

*"[Unborn children] qualify for protection unless and until we can be certain they are **not** live human persons."*

In the following viewpoint author Eugene F. Diamond argues that fetuses are indeed live humans and should be protected as such. The U.S. Supreme Court decision in *Roe v. Wade*, Diamond explains, stated that fetuses are not separate from their mothers but a part of them and therefore abortion should be legal. Fetuses do not have rights, the Court decided. Diamond states that this argument is flawed since fetuses are undeniably alive and human, and American society protects all other live humans. Eugene F. Diamond is a professor of pediatrics and a fellow at the Center for Bioethics and Human Dignity.

AS YOU READ, CONSIDER THE FOLLOWING QUESTIONS:

1. What did the 1973 Supreme Court decision in *Roe v. Wade* uphold?
2. Name one of the three reasons the author gives for assuming fetuses are independently alive.
3. Using the context of the paragraph in the fourth section of the essay, define *quandary*.

Eugene F. Diamond, "An Open Letter to the Open Minded," *Fellowship of Catholic Scholars Quarterly,* vol. 27, winter 2004. Reproduced by permission.

E very abortion decision involves a conflict of values. The rights of the developing unborn child are in conflict with the rights of the pregnant woman. Every physician who cares for pregnant women is caring for two patients—the pregnant woman herself and the unborn child. The pregnant woman frequently is called upon to act in a way that primarily is oriented toward the welfare of her unborn child. She may be asked to optimize her diet, abstain from smoking, or drink alcohol in moderation to protect her fetus. She may even be called upon to submit to procedures such as intrauterine transfusion or various fetal surgical measures to improve the condition of the infant without producing any direct benefit to herself. There is some disagreement about the ethical obligations of the mother in each instance, but few would claim that a mother may act with callous disregard for the welfare of the fetus. No one would claim for example,

Some antiabortion protesters use photos of aborted fetuses for shock value.

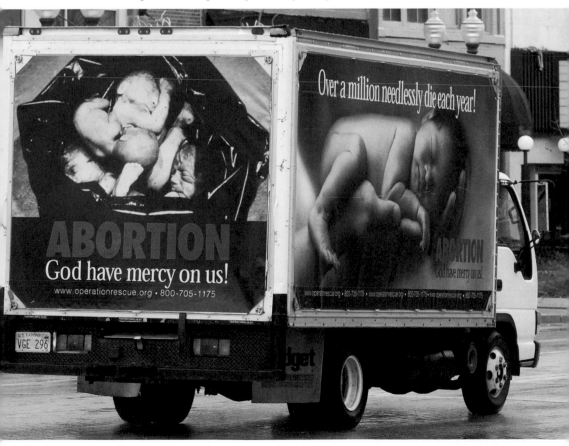

that a woman is free to take Thalidomide [an anti-nausea drug that causes birth detects] during the first trimester [three months] of pregnancy.

The Supreme Court Declared a Fetus Not a Person

The legalization of abortion [upheld by the Supreme Court in the 1973 *Roe v. Wade* decision] was based on a constitutional right to privacy, but it was contingent [dependent] on a declaration by the Court that the pre-viable fetus lacked personhood. It should be emphasized that the Court was discussing "personhood" in the legal sense of standing before the Court. It was not considering person-hood in a broader philosophical or metaphysical sense and, in fact, specifically refrained from a decision as to when life begins.

Fetuses Are Alive Independently from Their Mothers

The existence of biologically independent life in the unborn from the time of conception is supported by the following observations:

- Human life can be made to begin under in-vitro conditions [in a laboratory] by the fertilization of an ovum [egg] by sperm.

- The zygote [fertilized egg] and embryo thus produced are inde-pendently viable and not "part-of" the Petri dish or the uterus into which they will be eventually implanted.

- Criteria widely recognized as characteristic of "life" rather than "death" (e.g., heartbeat) are present early in the first trimester.

Unborn children have a unique dependency on their mothers, and they will continue to be totally dependent on others long after they are born. . . .

We Must Assume Fetuses Are People

If we conclude that when life begins is uncertain, we have a serious quandary. If we conclude that a human life or a human person does

Abortion Rights Around the World

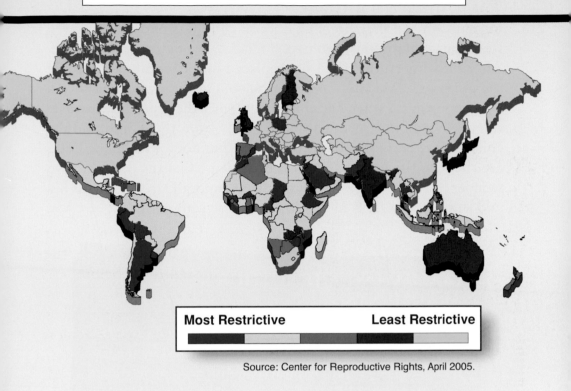

Most Restrictive   **Least Restrictive**

Source: Center for Reproductive Rights, April 2005.

not exist until some arbitrary stage of life after conception (e.g., implantation, nervous system development, viability, or birth) we may feel free to carry out lethal measures against pre-born individuals against whom we have passed this judgment. If we are incorrect, there is no remedy for the individual who has thus suffered wrongful death. If, on the other hand, we extend protection to all stages in the human continuum, we avoid the wrongful death without causing any injustice to the unborn individual in the process. It has been customary in other contexts in the American experience to act in favor of life where the existence of life is uncertain. When there is a coalmine cave-in, for example, we do not board up the shaft but rather we dig for survivors. In almost every instance, we continue to dig even when we are morally convinced that the oxygen supply has been long exhausted. It would seem reasonable to act similarly with regard to unborn children. That is, presume that they qualify for protection unless and until we can be certain that they are *not* live human persons.

Roe v. Wade Is a Mistake

Recently, in San Francisco, an unborn child was partially removed from the womb in order to have a renal tract obstruction repaired. After the surgery, the child was replaced in the womb to continue the pregnancy. Was this a person while out of the womb and then a non-person again when back inside? Or, since the procedure involves the removal of the lower half of the body from the womb, did the child achieve personhood for its buttocks but not for its brain? These are the scientific anomalies of the Supreme Court's decision. No wonder [former Supreme Court] Justice Sandra Day O'Connor has said that *Roe v. Wade* is on a collision course with itself.

EVALUATING THE AUTHOR'S ARGUMENTS:

In the viewpoint you just read, the author argues that because fetuses are alive, they should be protected by the law from harm as people are protected. American society does not allow the killing of humans. Therefore abortion should not be legal, he states. Do you agree with his argument or disagree? In your opinion, is a fetus a part of its mother or is it a separate being? Explain your reasoning.

Abortion Can Be Ethical

Cheryl Alkon

"I appreciate that life starts early in the womb, but also believe that I'm ending it for good reasons."

In the following first-person essay an obstetrician-gynecologist explains the reason that she continues to perform abortions. Abortion is simply a decision for the woman to make, she says. Many times, it is the right decision. Having another child may diminish the quality of life for the woman's existing children, or having an abortion may save the woman's life. Ending the life of the fetus is right and ethical, the doctor states, if it is done for the right reasons. The narrator of this essay chose to remain anonymous because of violent attacks on doctors who perform abortions.

AS YOU READ, CONSIDER THE FOLLOWING QUESTIONS:

1. What event made the doctor change her mind about performing abortions?

2. When are the "good days" to which the doctor refers?

3. What is one "good reason" the doctor gives for ending a pregnancy?

One morning years ago, when I was working as a resident, a nurse brought me in to talk to a pregnant girl. When I walked into the room, there was this child—an 11-year-old. She had

Cheryl Alkon, "Confessions of an Abortion Doctor," *Boston Magazine*, December 2004, copyright 2004 Metro Corp. All rights reserved. Reproduced by permission.

come in for a procedure, and it soon became obvious that she had no understanding of sex—she didn't really understand that she'd even had it, or that it had any connection to her pregnancy. We literally had to teach this girl about what it means to have sex—about STDs, abstinence, and pregnancy. I remember thinking: In a world where people don't want kids to learn about these things, how can you not give them the choice to terminate a pregnancy? Even if she had chosen to continue the pregnancy and opt for adoption, what would that have done to her own childhood? How can we not provide a child with any education about sex, then force her to become a parent long before she's ready?

Views on Abortion Can Change

When I started medical school in upstate New York, I didn't want to do terminations of pregnancies at all. My mom is Catholic and my dad is Jewish, and the church we went to had a pretty strong stance on it: The message I got was that abortion was wrong. As a first-year medical student, I took an ethics class and we talked about abortion. I wrote a paper about how I believed in the right, but would never perform an abortion myself, because it was against the way I was brought up.

That all changed later on, when I had a crush on this guy who was a leader of Medical Students for Choice. At the time, I thought abortion was strictly a women's issue. But he convinced me that abortion is a civil rights issue, that if you have injustice for some members of your population, your whole population has injustice. I remember thinking that was really profound. Still, I told him that I didn't feel comfortable doing abortions, but I was pro-choice. So he gave me these two films to watch, and they changed my life. They were about different providers and patients, men and women, who talked about what life was like before abortion was legal. They really changed my views—I suddenly thought, Yeah, I have to do that.

Doing Abortions Is Emotionally Taxing

Today, though, there are so few providers who will perform terminations that the people who do agree to provide them end up taking the bulk of procedures. It can be hard. I'm a generalist—I like a lot of different things about being an OB-GYN [obstetrician-gynecologist]. But because sometimes I'm the only person around, I end up doing a lot of terminations.

Planned Parenthood is a key figure in the abortion debate. The organization advocates for expanded access to abortion services like those it provides at clinics nationwide.

Doing them over and over and over again can be really taxing. All of us who provide abortions believe in what we're doing and think it's a good thing and a right that needs to be available. But when you're in the clinic and in that group of people doing it, it can be tough, and you can get really tired. I don't think it'll ever make me stop doing terminations, but it can move people to tears. And it's not just me—it extends to the nurses and the people who help us in the operating room. It's not unusual that you'll have only a couple of nurses who will help you out with it. There are nurses that will say, "No, I won't help you take care of this patient." I even know people who feel they can't tell their families what they do; their families think they work on labor and delivery.

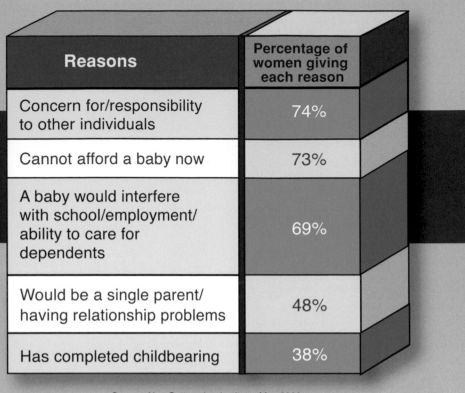

Reasons Given for Abortion

Reasons	Percentage of women giving each reason
Concern for/responsibility to other individuals	74%
Cannot afford a baby now	73%
A baby would interfere with school/employment/ability to care for dependents	69%
Would be a single parent/having relationship problems	48%
Has completed childbearing	38%

Source: Alan Guttmacher Institute, May 2006.

Abortion Can Be Right and Ethical

As providers, we give all options, including adoption and carrying the child to term. I always ask a patient, "Are you sure about this?" I've had people change their minds, which is totally okay. We want that. Or sometimes we'll advise them that they have more time to decide what to do. I would feel worse terminating a wanted child than not being able to terminate at all. It's very important that a woman knows what she wants to do either way. I have no problem with a woman walking out. I always find those are good days—when a woman walks out and says, "No, I'm keeping it."

I have the utmost respect for life; I appreciate that life starts early in the womb, but also believe that I'm ending it for good reasons. Often I'm saving the woman, or I'm improving the lives of the other children in the family. I also believe that women have a life they have to consider. If a woman is working full-time, has one child already, and is barely getting by, having another child that would financially push her to go on public assistance is going to lessen the quality of her life. And it's also an issue for the child, if it would not have had a good life. Life's hard enough when you're wanted and everything's prepared for. So yes, I end life, but even when it's hard, it's for a good reason. . . .

Maybe I live in an idealistic world, but I believe in people being good and in trying to understand their opinion. I don't think I'm going to be easily swayed. Obviously, the threat of violence is something that's always in the back of my mind, that it could happen, but I feel like I'm doing something so right. How could people think it's wrong?

EVALUATING THE AUTHORS' ARGUMENTS:

In the essay you just read, the doctor believes that abortion should be a woman's own decision. In the previous essay, Eugene F. Diamond states that the government should decide if a woman is permitted to have an abortion or not. Which argument do you agree with? Should the government decide what a woman should do with her body, or should the woman herself decide?

A Fetus Is a Person

Jonathan Gurwitz

"A child ripped from its mother's womb at eight months cannot be a victim while the same child crushed in a surgical procedure is not."

In the following viewpoint author Jonathan Gurwitz argues that by calling those still in the womb fetuses and those outside of the womb babies, abortion supporters make it easier to abort the unborn children. However, more advanced ultrasounds that show distinct pictures of the unborn are making this distinction more difficult, Gurwitz states. The photographs reveal very human-looking babies. All those conceived, whether born or unborn, are babies, in the opinion of the author, and should be treated as such. Jonathan Gurwitz is a columnist who writes on conservative issues for the *San Antonio Express-News*.

AS YOU READ, CONSIDER THE FOLLOWING QUESTIONS:

1. What word does the author believe best describes unborn children?

2. What new technology is making people in the pro-choice movement uncomfortable, according to the author?

3. What did Frances Kissling, president of Catholics for Free Choice, tell pro-choice activists that they need to reconsider?

A new industry has developed around the ultrasound technology used as a diagnostic tool in medicine. Parents-to-be are having vanity ultrasound portraits taken of their unborn children. In fact, so many people are now taking "pre-baby" photos—and so many unregulated "studios" are popping up to offer the service—that doctors groups and the Food and Drug Administration have issued warnings about the dangers of ultrasound misuse.

Ultrasound is peeling back the curtain on the unrevealed child in utero [in the womb]. Or, as some people will choose to refer to it, a fetus. Medical technology, at the same time, is rendering obsolete much of the language of the abortion debate.

The Difference Between a Baby and a Fetus

How does one know if an unborn child is a baby or a fetus?

The question was highlighted by a gruesome crime that took place in Missouri [in December 2004]. Authorities have charged Lisa

Virginia legislator Richard H. Black presents a "fetal pain" bill to his state's senate in 2005. Had it passed, the bill would have provided anesthesia prior to an abortion for a fetus over the age of twenty weeks.

Montgomery with strangling Bobbie Jo Stinnett, who was eight months pregnant.

Montgomery, however, did more. According to one Associated Press report, she's also accused of "cutting out the fetus and taking the baby."

Ponder that feat of linguistic gymnastics. Was Stinnett pregnant with one child—the fetus—and Montgomery took another child—the baby? Or was there only one child involved and some transformative event occurred in the instant between being cut out and taken?

The answer, of course, is neither. There was only one child, but no transformative event. The child, a girl, was as much a baby be-

When Does Human Life Begin?

Do you believe that human life begins at conception, or once the baby may be able to survive outside the mother's womb with medical assistance, or when the baby is actually born?

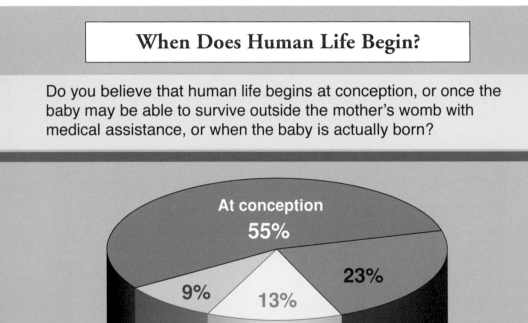

At conception
55%

23%

9%

13%

Not
sure

At birth

Baby
survives
outside
of womb

Source: Fox News / Opinion Dynamics Poll, July 15–16, 2003.

fore she was cut from her mother's womb as after. Miraculously, she survived and eventually was reunited with her father.

Ultrasound Makes Pro-Abortion Arguments Difficult
Prebirth ultrasounds and the archaic reasoning revealed in the Stinnett murder make some people in the pro-choice movement distinctly uncomfortable. For them, anything that might confer babyhood on a fetus, anything that might affect people's perceptions about an unrestricted policy of abortion on demand is viewed as a threat.

Frances Kissling, president of Catholics for Free Choice, told pro-choice activists they need to reconsider "the value of the fetus." In the winter [2004] issue of [*Conscience*] magazine, she observed the political consequences of "what appears to be an absolute right to abortion that brooks no consideration of other values."

FAST FACT

In 2005 Congress agreed that a fetus is a person by passing the Unborn Victims of Violence Act, which makes a fetus a separate crime victim if a pregnant woman is killed.

"As the fetus has become more visible through both antiabortion efforts and advances in fetal medicine," Kissling admonished, "this stance has become less satisfying as either a moral framework or a message strategy."

All Unborn Children Are Babies
People who are framing ultrasound photos of their unborn children will not succumb to the notion that their lives are a matter of "choice."

A child ripped from its mother's womb at eight months cannot be a victim while the same child crushed in a surgical procedure is not. The act of being "wanted" does not confer life.

Parents keeping vigils in neo-natal intensive care units will not accept that at 26 weeks of gestation a child is not "viable."

Just more than six years ago, my son was born three months early. In the course of a few hours of panic and unanswered prayers, he arrived dangerously prematurely, just over two pounds and 15 inches long.

In desperate situations, people look for the most inconsequential signs of hope. As an avid fisherman, I knew that the legal minimum to keep a speckled trout, a prized game fish in Texas, was 15 inches. As painful as that mental comparison was, I tried to hearten myself by saying, "He's a keeper."

After months of intensive care from exceptional doctors and staff, my son came home, our prayers answered. Today he is a perfectly healthy boy.

At some hospitals and clinics, however, he would not have been a keeper. In fact, he would not have been a baby.

EVALUATING THE AUTHOR'S ARGUMENTS:

In the viewpoint you just read, the author states that people—namely, pro-choice activists—have manipulated language in order to make unborn children seem less human. Calling an unborn child a fetus makes abortion easier than if the unborn child was called a baby. Do you agree that the way in which people use certain words can manipulate meanings? Why or why not?

A Fetus Is Not a Person

Patricia J. Williams

"There is, these days, a tendency to conceive of the fetus as an entire person, and a litigious little person at that."

In this article from the *Nation* magazine, law professor Patricia J. Williams points out that now that people can see the fetus in the mother's womb with modern technology, the fetus is no longer seen as a part of the mother's body, as it has been historically. Instead, the fetus is seen as a whole, separate person with its own desires and feelings. Moreover, the author points out, even embryos, which are clumps of cells, are beginning to be seen as beings that have emotions and desires and must not be destroyed via abortion. This view has confused the idea of what constitutes a person and dangerously deflects attention from those who need it most: the children already born who are poor or in need of adoption.

AS YOU READ, CONSIDER THE FOLLOWING QUESTIONS:

1. What has made the fetus seem a separate being from the woman carrying it?
2. When did the president of Arizona Right to Life say that life begins?
3. What concern arises when cellular life is equated with personhood, according to the author?

In the beginning, there was a time when doctors treated pregnant women by listening to them tell of their symptoms. There were no visuals, no color glossies, no T-shirts with the sonogram emblazoned. There was relative quiet in the womb, which took quiet to attend to. It required listening to the woman say, "This is what it feels like." It required a palpating of the body, a laying on of hands. Midwives and doctors used touch, eyes, ears, measuring from the outside to get a sense of what was within—sounds, motions, clues. It was the mother-to-be whose health was indicative of the condition of the embryo or fetus. Whether life was deemed to begin at conception or whether with quickening, the interdependence of the womb and the woman was a given. I'm certainly not advocating that we turn back the clock with regard to obstetric medicine, but it is arresting to recall that intercon-

Signe Wilkinson Editorial Cartoon © 1989 Signe Wilkinson. All rights reserved. Used with permission of Signe Wilkinson and the Washington Post Writers Group in conjunction with the Cartoonist Group. Published originally in the *Philadelphia Daily News*.

nectedness in a time when "life" has become increasingly divorced from traditional contours of the human body. We live in a time when embryos and fetuses are gaining legal rights to sue, are attaining the status of persons, are being enshrined in a molecularly sized iconography of innocents to be saved. With technology, we can make visual what no generation has been privy to before. Like satellites homing in on a secret bunker from space, we have the spyware to case the joint—the interior of the uterus, the cells, even mitochondria, and now DNA.

Fetuses Have Become People

With all that comes interpretation, and politics, and ideology. And lo, the birth of "the unborn." The magnified fetus becomes an external, a separate entity. Women are no longer imbued with the halo-illuminated metaphors of ripeness and enfolding that underscore so many of our religious notions about women round with child. At least or perhaps especially in the United States, we find ourselves tangled in new definitions of separation and individuation. There has been a restructuring, of our rhetoric as well as of certain religious ideologies, that expressly pits a woman's body against her fetus. There is, these days, a tendency to conceive of the fetus as an entire person, and a litigious [argumentative] little person at that, with a warrior attitude and a long list of complaints that can be asserted against the madonna in question. We've all read about negligence actions, criminal cases, child welfare cases, all involving fetuses still *in utero*. But the status of the fetus is no longer the most contentious part of the debate. It's moved further and further back in the developmental cycle. Recently the Arizona court of appeals declined to rule that a set of cryogenically frozen fertilized eggs were "persons" for purposes of a wrongful death action, saying that such a designation was for the legislature. The lawsuit was brought by a couple who had sued the Mayo Clinic after its lab lost or possibly destroyed some of the eggs. The eggs were days old, still a clump of cells; nevertheless the court was careful to craft a special category for

FAST FACT

Doctors generally agree that the earliest a fetus can survive outside the womb is twenty-three weeks. Full-term gestation is thirty-seven weeks.

them: "pre-embryos." Pre-embryonic status is thus not a biological designation but rather a new legal category, a way of dodging the political controversy engendered by those who believe embryos are calling out for rescue. As John Jacubczyk, president of Arizona Right to Life, stated the argument: "Life begins at fertilization."

Embryos Seen as Having Feelings

Although the Arizona court did not confer personhood in this case, the matter is sure to be appealed; furthermore, an Illinois court ruled this past February [2005] that an embryo is a person, a claim that is likely to make its way to higher authorities—whether courts or legislatures—sometime in the not so distant future. So we should consider carefully the collective narratives that are shaping the debates. At one end we have the Snowflakes Frozen Embryo Adoption Program, a Christian organization that has made it its mission to rescue the unused embryos that have been harvested by fertility clinics and then discarded by couples once they do achieve a successful pregnancy. Snowflakes considers the abandonment and/or destruction of those cells nothing less than murder, and so has set out to "adopt" discarded embryos. It has rounded up women in whom to implant them, and families with whom to place the babies thus brought to term. Mere blastemas [a clump of cells] are imbued with intent and longing; indeed, the Snowflakes website asserts that it is "helping some of the more than 400,000 frozen embryos reach their ultimate purpose—life."

Cells Are Given Personhood

On the other side of things there is a philosophically inflected concern that if cellular "life" is equated with personhood, and personhood begins at fertilization, then the very notion of the person as an autonomous entity becomes terribly vexed. Eggs fertilized in a petri dish and stored in a freezer are more consistent with our notions of property, of product, of artifice. From this angle, eggs in a dish are relatively artificial, a species of mechanical construct requiring tools, inventory, technology. At the same time, there is also a commercial narrative of altruism, in which those fertilized eggs are, not unlike the Snowflakes website's take, so purposeful, so hyper-autonomous, that they can fight their way out of a petri dish with no help from a

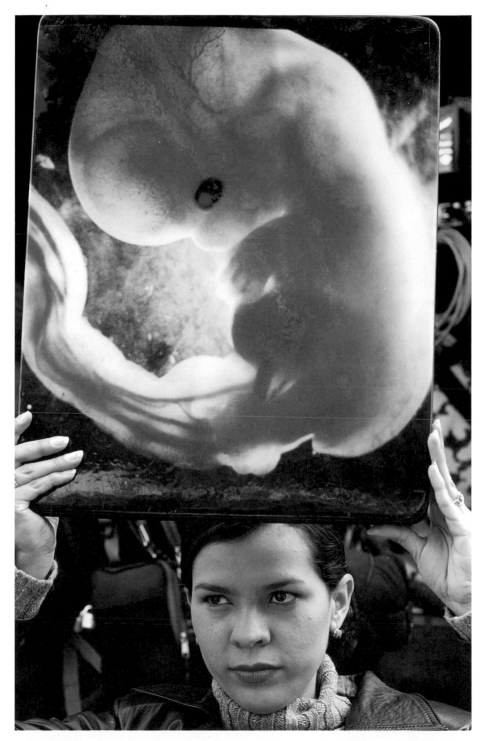

Some antiabortion protesters use photos like these of fetuses in the womb to attempt to counteract the belief that a fetus is not a person.

womb or a woman or even a mad scientist. Personhood becomes an anthropomorphizing of cellular life—the tiny but strong, the minuscule but mighty, the intelligence with design, the responsible agent, the genie in the jar that imprisons the fully formed perfect child yearning to break free. It is a very seductive story, even if it is questionable as a scientific matter. And more to the point for us in the legal community, it confuses will and determinism, potential and predestination.

Don't Forget Children Already Born

But if the power of these narratives has resulted in a kind of cult celebrity status for the pre-born, or prenatal, or pre-conscious or whatever, imagine how much more creative it will get with the emerging overlays of DNA screening, of accumulating commercial interests in profiles for health insurance, in DNA banks as a tool of social engineering. Somewhere between the extremities of the moment, we must remember that there is nothing inevitable in this course; let us not be seduced by an idealized personification of destiny. Let us not forget that one in five American children lives in poverty. And at least 130,000 post-born, not-so-perfect children ("surplus" is how Seventh Circuit Judge Richard Posner once expressed it) are available for domestic adoption at any given time. Aren't they "a person" too?

EVALUATING THE AUTHORS' ARGUMENTS:

In the viewpoint you just read by Patricia J. Williams and the preceding one by Jonathan Gurwitz, both of the authors agree that fetuses and even embryos are being increasingly seen as people separate from the women who carry them. However, Gurwitz believes this new view is correct, and Williams disagrees. With which author do you agree? Do you believe that fetuses and embryos should be considered people with rights? Or are they a part of their mother until they are born? Explain your answer.

Roe v. Wade Should Be Overturned

Jan LaRue

"The lionization of [Roe v. Wade] as untouchable precedent . . . rests on the fallacy that we do not know when life begins."

The landmark 1973 Supreme Court decision *Roe v. Wade* upheld the right to abortion. In the following viewpoint the author argues that *Roe v. Wade* should be overturned because its declaration that a fetus is not a person is based on faulty logic. The Fourteenth Amendment of the Constitution provides for equal protection under the law for all people in the nation, the author points out. Harry Blackmun, the Supreme Court Justice who wrote the *Roe* decision, used shaky reasoning to determine that fetuses are not people and therefore not entitled to protection under the Fourteenth Amendment. *Roe v. Wade* is not a valid decision, the author argues. Jan LaRue is the chief attorney for the conservative lobbying group Concerned Women for America.

AS YOU READ, CONSIDER THE FOLLOWING QUESTIONS:

1. What does LaRue call "one of the greatest suppressions of truth in Supreme Court history?"
2. What are three qualities the author names that prove the unborn are alive at conception?

Jan LaRue, "It's Time to Reject *Roe v. Wade* as an Invincible Precedent," November 22, 2005. www.cwfa.org. Reproduced by permission.

A U.S. senator appeared on a news show [in] early [November 2005] to discuss his meeting with Supreme Court nominee Judge Samuel Alito. The topic naturally turned to abortion. The senator said his religious belief is that human life begins at conception. He expressed his hope that someday science will actually tell us when human life begins.

The senator is pro-life, yet he missed a great opportunity to speak the truth. We know when life begins but the tragedy is that our abor-

The key legislative decision in the abortion debate is the 1973 Supreme Court ruling in Roe v. Wade *that made abortion legal. Abortion opponents seek to have this judgment overturned.*

tion laws are based on one of the greatest suppressions of truth in Supreme Court history, otherwise known as *Roe v. Wade.*

The lionization of *Roe* as untouchable precedent, which has become the definitive litmus test for Supreme Court nominees, rests on the fallacy that we do not know when life begins. The myth stems from seven Supreme Court justices who decided that it was unnecessary to know when life begins in order to decide if it may be ended. After implying that judges aren't smart enough to even guess when life begins, the seven decided to decide anyway.

The majority's predetermined outcome exposes an activist court willing to adopt a ridiculous rationale in order to create a new "constitutional right."

Fetuses Not Protected by Constitution

In his preparation to write the majority opinion in *Roe v. Wade*, the late Supreme Court Justice Harry Blackmun spent an entire summer studying the international history of abortion law and reading textbooks in the Mayo Clinic medical library.

Blackmun identified the salient [prominent] issue that stood in the way of *Roe* prevailing on the theory that abortion is a constitutional right. He wrote, "If this suggestion of personhood (fetus) is established, the appellant's [one appealing a court decision] case, of course, collapses, for the fetus' right to life would then be guaranteed by the [14th] Amendment."

In order to deny the unborn status as "persons" protected by the 14th Amendment [which provides for equal protection under the law for all people], the Court first had to dehumanize them. The majority did so by pretending that no one could agree on when human life begins. . . .

And it gets worse. The unborn, Blackmun decreed with a straight face, are merely "potential life" until "viability," the time when "the fetus becomes 'viable,' that is, potentially able to live outside the mother's womb, albeit with artificial aid." Not subject to cross-examination, Blackmun wasn't made to explain how "potential life," i.e., non-life, is capable of development. . . .

Put simply, rotten meat doesn't produce the maggots crawling on it nor are mice produced by the pile of rags on which they crawl. All life comes from pre-existing life. There is no period of nonlife.

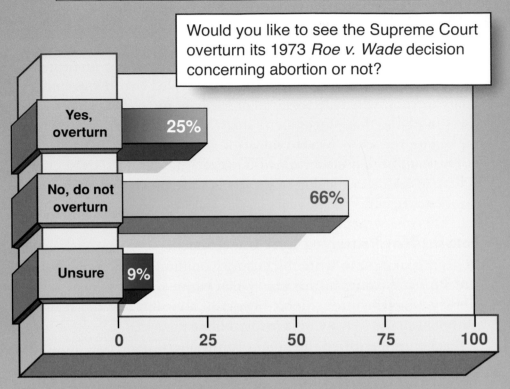

Twenty-Five Percent of Americans Favor Overturning *Roe v. Wade*

Would you like to see the Supreme Court overturn its 1973 *Roe v. Wade* decision concerning abortion or not?

Yes, overturn — 25%

No, do not overturn — 66%

Unsure — 9%

| 0 | 25 | 50 | 75 | 100 |

Source: CNN / *USA Today* / Gallup Poll, January 20–22, 2006.

Biological growth—metabolism, reproduction and reaction to stimuli —proves the unborn are alive at conception. They are human life because each being reproduces after its own kind. It is nonsensical to conclude that two human beings produce a being that later becomes a human being. . . .

Unborn Not Included in 14th Amendment

With the first linchpin pulled out from protection for the unborn, Blackmun proceeded to pull the second. He concluded that no case had been cited that included the fetus within the language of the 14th Amendment. The fact that no case existed that included a right to abortion under any provision of the Constitution didn't stop Blackmun from creating the one that did. . . .

Blackmun argued that the reference to "person" in the 14th Amendment means "citizens" who are born or naturalized in the

United States. "All this together with our observation . . . persuades us that the word *person* does not include the unborn." The fact that aliens, who are neither born in the U.S. nor naturalized, are persons protected by the Amendment was of no moment to Blackmun.

Blackmun arbitrarily refused to include the unborn in the doctrine of "personhood," even though "person" in the 14th Amendment includes inanimate entities such as corporations and ships. Blackmun's conclusion went further than the 14th Amendment: "In short, the unborn have never been recognized in the law as persons in the whole sense.". . .

Same Protection for Mother and Fetus

Blackmun and six other highly educated men agreed that it didn't matter whether the unborn are human life in order to decide

A well-known antiabortion display is the field of white crosses, each representing an aborted fetus.

whether they can be terminated without due process. It's no wonder that Justice Byron White called it an act of "raw judicial power."

It is wrong, however, to state that *Roe* actually holds that the unborn are not human beings. Furthermore, consider the following [example] of legal protection for the unborn, both pre- and post-*Roe*:

> The unborn child in the path of an automobile is as much a person in the street as the mother. The criminal law regards it as a separate entity and the law of property considers it in being for all purposes which are to its benefit, such as, taking by will or descent. He may maintain an action for prenatal injuries and if he dies of such injuries, an action will lie for his wrongful death. . . .
>
> Legal fictions that attempt to distinguish between a fetus and a human being, and yet impose the same penalty for murdering either, expose a flawed and dangerous policy in which the unborn's right to life depends on who wants it terminated—the mother or another. . . .
>
> And what does it say about a nation that protects the nests and eggs of endangered species to the same degree that it protects them as adults but fails to protect the life of unborn humans?

EVALUATING THE AUTHOR'S ARGUMENTS:

In a famous nineteenth-century Supreme Court case, *Dred Scott v. Sandford*, the justices decided that slaves were not people to be protected under the Constitution. This case is frequently compared with *Roe v. Wade*, which states that fetuses are also not people who are afforded protection. Do you think this is a fair comparison? Give your reasons.

Roe v. Wade Should Be Preserved

Chicago Sun-Times

"We need to remember women have a right to govern their own bodies."

In the following editorial from the *Chicago Sun-Times*, the editorial staff argues that despite the presence of *Roe v. Wade*, women are steadily losing their rights to abortion. Both state and federal governments have passed laws that make it more difficult for doctors to provide abortions and women to pay for them. Private organizations also are pressuring women publicly not to get abortions. Yet abortion rights are essential to women's health and safety and must be upheld, the authors state. Women who are prevented from legally obtaining abortions will only seek dangerous, illegal ones. Thus banning abortion will not solve the problem.

AS YOU READ, CONSIDER THE FOLLOWING QUESTIONS:

1. What does the Hyde Amendment of 1977 prohibit?
2. What percentage of U.S. counties had no abortion provider as of 2000?
3. What are the two best ways to prevent abortion, according to the authors?

One image shows a 12-week-old fetus yawning. The other shows the fetus "walking," moving its legs through the amniotic fluid. The images were the clearest ever taken of a first trimester fetus, captured with a special ultrasound by a British obstetrician and published in the *Sun-Times* on Wednesday. Someone in our office pointed to the pictures and asked: "What's this going to do to the abortion debate?"

The early fetal images did look "baby-like," less amorphous than previous ultrasounds had, and the question made us pause. Would these kinds of pictures make a woman who sought to end a pregnancy feel more guilty about her decision?

Abortion Is a Difficult Decision

Looking at these pictures is complicated because abortion is complicated—no one has ever said it is a happy way to end a preg-

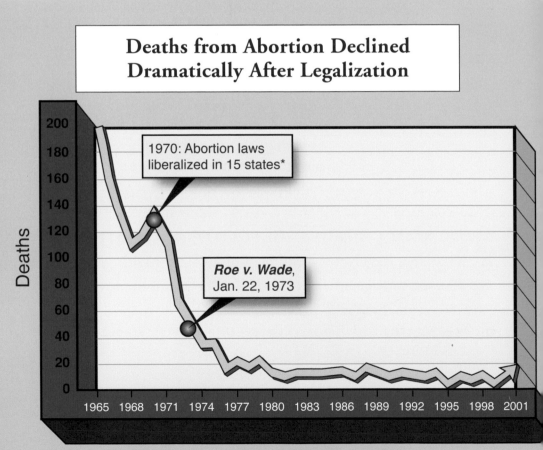

Deaths from Abortion Declined Dramatically After Legalization

1970: Abortion laws liberalized in 15 states*

Roe v. Wade, Jan. 22, 1973

Note: *By the end of 1970, four states had repealed their antiabortion laws, and eleven states had reformed them.

Source: The Alan Guttmacher Institute, May 2006.

Abortion supporters seek to preserve the decision handed down in Roe v. Wade.

nancy. No one who has ever had an abortion can forget the deep loneliness of her decision, the doubt and anxiety, the fear and anguish. No one, not the foolish teen who in the passion of the moment didn't think about birth control or the married woman who is carrying a child with life-threatening birth defects. It is only the absolutist anti-abortion groups and absolutist pro-abortion groups who are able to evince such moral certitude about it. Most Americans who are moderate and pro-choice always have questions.

Abortion Rights Disintegrating

What is certain is that since the *Roe vs. Wade* decision in 1973, which upheld women's right to privacy—giving them the possibility of choice—abortion rights have been chipped away bit by bit. There is the "Hyde Amendment" (1977) which prohibits Medicaid funding for abortion. There are TRAP laws in 35 states that subject abortion providers to more stringent medical and administrative requirements than other clinics, making it more difficult for them to offer abortions. It's harder to even get an abortion these days: 87 percent of

U.S counties had no abortion provider in 2000. And, fewer doctors are being trained to do the procedure.

Besides the legal impediments, there are psychological ones. There is the pressure from the Catholic Church and fundamentalist groups. There is harassment by picketers outside abortion clinics. There is the violence: bombings, arsons and murder. Remember Dr. Bernard Slepian who was killed in 1998 as he stood in his kitchen in Amherst, N.Y.?

Roe vs. Wade was upheld by the Supreme Court in 1992 but the reason 1.5 million women marched in Washington last April was their fear that this right will incrementally disappear. They were thinking about laws such as the Partial-Birth Abortion Ban Act, or the Unborn Victims of Violence Act, which aims to protect the fetus and embryo. The Washington marchers wanted to remind everyone that a woman's right to abortion is still protected by the Supreme Court and endorsed by the majority of Americans.

Abortion supporters hold a candlelight vigil in front of the Supreme Court building in Washington, D.C.

Banning Abortion Won't Stop It

The truth is that since 1994, abortion has been declining. Better access to birth control and better sex education are the fundamental reasons. Ninety percent of abortions are performed during the first trimester and the majority of women who seek one are not using it as a form of birth control. "If a sexually active woman were to use abortion as her means of birth control and wanted two children, she would have about 30 abortions by the time she reached age 45," according to a recent study by the Alan Guttmacher Institute. The women most in need of abortion rights are poor, black and Hispanic. Women who lack health insurance or are under Medicaid are unable to pay for an abortion. In the first year the Hyde Amendment was enacted, about 2,000 Medicaid women sought abortions without a doctor, according to the NARAL Pro-Choice America Foundation.

Preventing abortions would not end the issue, it would just make it dangerous and tragic. When we look at these ultrasounds of fetuses, we need to remember women have a right to govern their own bodies. The best way to prevent abortion is to continue to support sex education and allow easy access to birth control. These are the only answers. Fundamentally, abortion is a very personal issue.

EVALUATING THE AUTHORS' ARGUMENTS:

Roe v. Wade is the most controversial decision in Supreme Court history. The authors of the viewpoint you just read feel that a woman's right to govern her own body should be protected under the law. The author of the previous viewpoint feels that protecting the unborn fetus should be the priority of the law. Which view do you agree with? Explain your answer.

Chapter 2

What Restrictions Should Be Placed on Abortion?

Abortion legislation is frequently debated at both the state and federal level.

Aborting a Fetus with Disabilities Should Be Discouraged

Deborah Kendrick

Deborah Kendrick is a writer who is blind. In the following viewpoint she points out that abortions of fetuses with potential disabilities have increased in America as technology to detect disabling conditions has improved. Kendrick writes that as a person with a disability, she was subtly encouraged to abort her fetus, which may have inherited her condition. These eugenic abortions must be discouraged, she writes. Sanctioning eugenic abortions gives the false impression that not all life is worth living. Many people with disabilities live full and productive lives, Kendrick argues, and her own life is an example.

"Eugenic abortions ... are on the rise in America, and no one's talking about it."

AS YOU READ, CONSIDER THE FOLLOWING QUESTIONS:

1. To what regime does Kendrick compare the rise in eugenic abortions?

2. What is the "other end of the human continuum" to which the author refers when discussing the case of Terri Schiavo?

3. What does Kendrick imply might have happened to her when she says "had the test been available when my mother was pregnant with me, I might not be here?"

My daughter is just about as complicated as a teenager can be. She can sleep all day and study all night. She writes poetry that takes your breath away. She's articulate, opinionated, hilarious and naive. She's terribly spoiled but incredibly generous and passionate about many ideals.

One issue in the abortion debate is the amount and nature of counseling that women receive when contemplating an abortion.

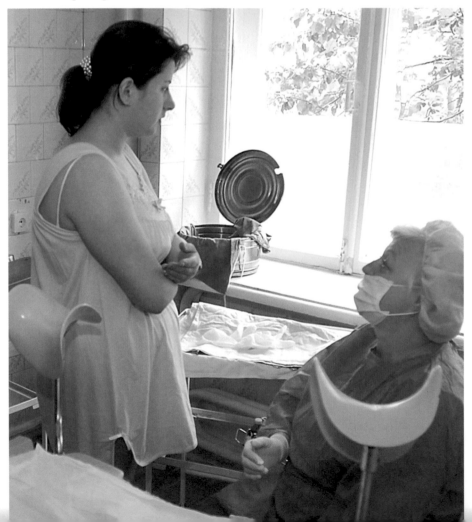

Two months before she was born, a physician told me that her birth was "unfortunate": The rare childhood cancer that resulted in blindness for me can be hereditary. I learned that just before my first child was born. I was traumatized.

Happily, I found a brilliant, compassionate ophthalmologist who changed all that. He piled my arms with literature and my heart with reassurances that treatment was significantly better than it had been in my childhood and that I, more than uninitiated parents, understood the possibilities. The disease occurs only in childhood, so, the first five years of each of my children's lives included frequent eye examinations. No one inherited the gene.

Lack of Support from Medical Community

But when my youngest child was about to be born, my doctor had left the state, and I consulted another. This younger physician told me that there would soon be a prenatal test for the gene, then added, with unmistakable disdain, "Unfortunately, it's too late for you."

I've never been sure of what he meant. Too late for me, a woman who should have been aborted? Or too late for my baby?

Months earlier, I had signed a waiver that said I had declined a prenatal test that might detect Down syndrome or spina bifida. "I never open my Christmas presents early," I had said.

But the wave of parents not only peeking at those presents early, but discarding them, is on the rise.

Eugenic Abortions Increasing

Eugenic abortions—eliminating babies because of such conditions as deafness, blindness, dwarfism, Down syndrome and more—are on the rise in America, and no one's talking about it. We can righteously decry the malevolence of Nazi Germany and remain oblivious to the truth that we're already following in Hitler's footsteps.

About 275,000 children and adults were murdered under Adolf Hitler's regime, many of them not meeting his Aryan criteria, because they had or were believed to have some physical or mental disability.

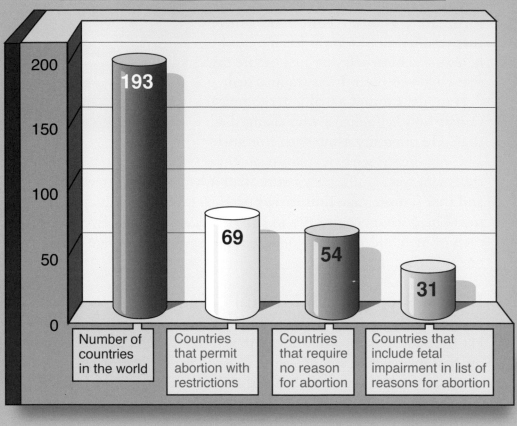

Number of Countries That Permit Abortion if Fetus Is Impaired

193	69	54	31
Number of countries in the world	Countries that permit abortion with restrictions	Countries that require no reason for abortion	Countries that include fetal impairment in list of reasons for abortion

Source: "The World's Abortion Laws," Center for Reproductive Rights, April 2005.

[In 2005] the *New England Journal of Medicine* reported on a project in the Netherlands in which 22 infants with spina bifida were euthanized. Some journalists erroneously referred to the dead babies as having had terminal diseases. Many people right here in Ohio have spina bifida and lead full, productive and happy lives.

And this separate standard applied to the value of life before birth—i.e., the notion that life with a disability is not worth living, so let's spare this kid from being born—is applied with equal or greater fervor at the other end of our human continuum.

Life with Disability Is Worth Living

We're coming up on the first anniversary of the death of Terri Schiavo, the Florida woman whose right to live or die was debated in court for years. When her feeding tube was removed, she took two weeks to die from starvation and dehydration.

[In January 2006], the Supreme Court voted 6–3 that Oregon can keep its assisted-suicide law, giving further credence to the concept that life with disability is life not worth living.

If my position on these issues seems uncharacteristic of other opinions expressed in this column, well, maybe it's because it's so personal. Had the test been available when my mother was pregnant with me, I might not be here.

My daughter is the light of my life. She doesn't know, unless she reads this, that a doctor once told me her birth shouldn't happen.

So the fact that she's on her way to Washington with several other teenagers to participate in the 33rd annual March for Life makes me, as a mother, very proud. And as a human being, it gives me hope for all of us.

EVALUATING THE AUTHOR'S ARGUMENTS:

In the viewpoint you just read, Deborah Kendrick compares the rise in abortions of fetuses with potential disabilities to Adolf Hitler's killing of people with disabilities during the Nazi regime. Do you think this is a fair comparison? In what ways does the current abortion trend resemble the Nazis' killing? In what ways does it differ?

Aborting a Fetus with Disabilities Should Be Permitted

Maria Eftimiades

"While I have no doubt there can be joys and victories in raising a mentally handicapped child . . . it's a painful journey [my boyfriend and I] believe is better not taken."

In the following viewpoint the author explains her personal experience aborting a fetus diagnosed with Down syndrome. She did not feel she was generally supported by society, she writes. She had to conceal her experience from some friends and family who might disapprove. The decision was painful and difficult, she acknowledges, but she was glad to have the option of a safe abortion. An abortion is an entirely personal matter, she emphasizes, and for her and her partner, it was the right one. Maria Eftimiades is a journalist who writes for *People* magazine.

AS YOU READ, CONSIDER THE FOLLOWING QUESTIONS:

1. What are the odds the author cites for having a baby with Down syndrome at the age of forty-two?
2. What do the author and her mother tell some people happened to the fetus?

"So when do you go for the abortion?" my friend asked, her voice sympathetic.

"Wednesday," I replied, and then hurriedly got off the phone. I called Mike, my boyfriend, in tears, complaining about how inconsiderate people are, how no one thinks before they speak. The truth was, until I heard the word "abortion," it hadn't occurred to me that I was actually having one.

News of Down Syndrome

I was, of course. But we'd been using euphemisms for days, ever since my doctor called to say my amniocentesis results "weren't good." We'd say "when we go to the hospital" or "the appointment" or "after the procedure, we can try again."

We were driving to the post office, Mike and I, near our home when my cell phone rang and I recognized the OB-GYN's number. I said, "It's the doctor," and then, a little later, "Oh, no." Mike pulled over and held my hand while I listened. It didn't take long; the doctor didn't have much to say. He suggested we digest the news and call him later.

When I hung up, I told Mike, "It's Down syndrome" and we went home and lay in bed for the rest of the day. We were shocked.

Planning for a Baby

Perhaps we shouldn't have been. I was a few weeks from my 42nd birthday. Mike was 52. This was to be the first child for both of us. We'd read the statistics: at my age, a 1-in-100 chance of a Down syndrome baby, although my doctor said later he'd put the figure closer to 1-in-40. Not the best odds, but somehow we never expected we'd be the couple to receive bad news.

When I first learned I was pregnant, I was thrilled yet guarded. It wasn't because I was afraid of a miscarriage—though I was. I worried about what I might hear, given that Mike and I weren't married, and had decided to wait before taking that step.

My family and close friends were delighted, but I found myself filing away insensitive remarks from those second-tier friends—a work colleague, a member of my softball team, a neighbor. Some examples: "It's Mike's, I assume?" "So, is this good news?" "Who's the father? Just kidding!" And my favorite: "How did it happen? No birth control?"

From the start of my pregnancy, I tried to be so careful. Mike brought home fresh fruit for me every evening, and I fretted when the pharmacy didn't have my prenatal vitamins in stock and I had to wait an extra day. I even wrote to Starbucks to request they add black decaffeinated tea to their menu. (Herbals aren't good for pregnant women.) Though we tried not to get too excited, Mike and I began searching for names—we even found ourselves studying the credits at the end of movies. For a girl, we were far apart; for a boy, we leaned toward John—we both have a brother with that name.

Concealing an Abortion

Once I had the amnio and saw from the sonogram it was a boy, I thought I was in the clear: It didn't occur to me to wait for the test

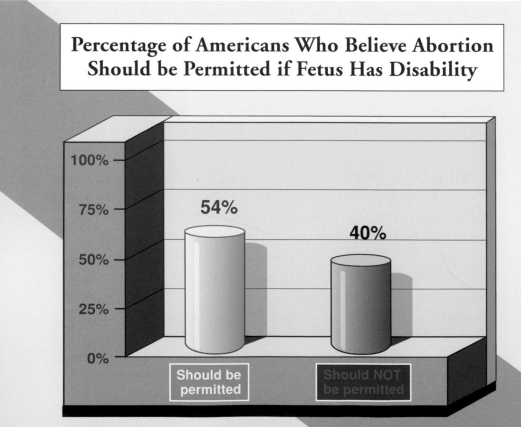

Percentage of Americans Who Believe Abortion Should be Permitted if Fetus Has Disability

Source: ABC News/*Washington Post* poll, January 22, 2004.

results before sharing the news more freely. One Sunday morning I told my softball friends I was pregnant and they cheered the prospect of a new player and told me I'd done the team well by producing a boy. The very next weekend, I stayed home from the game, devastated by my whirling misfortune.

Later, one of my teammates suggested that I tell others I had a miscarriage.

"You never know how people will react," he said.

My mother, too, was a proponent of the miscarriage story. She told two of my brothers the truth; she told the third that I'd suddenly lost the baby. That brother's wife was a Catholic, and my mother was taking no chances.

"People are funny," she said.

The Abortion Debate

I've heard the abortion debate my whole life, and while I was a newspaper reporter I had covered stories about clinic bombings and protests. I interviewed [antiabortion activist] Randall Terry of Operation Rescue when I was in my twenties. I talked with his supporters who stood outside clinics and imitated babies crying, begging "Mommy, don't kill me," when abortion-seekers passed by.

Once I became one of those women ending a pregnancy, I found myself wondering how I'd react under that kind of pressure. I remember a cop I interviewed once telling me about a "good rape," one where the attacker was a stranger and there was no ambiguity, no chance of blaming the victim because she had drunk too much or invited her date in for coffee. I wonder if it's the same for abortion. If your child will be born with a severe disability, is there a "Get Out of Jail Free" card or are you still a baby killer?

A Painful Decision

While I have no doubt there can be joys and victories in raising a mentally handicapped child, for me and for Mike, it's a painful journey that we believe is better not taken. To know now that our son would be retarded, perhaps profoundly, gives us the choice of not continuing the pregnancy. We don't want a life like that for our child, and the added worry that we wouldn't be around long enough to care for him throughout his life.

For some reason, I expected our baby would look like Mike— sandy-colored, silky hair, hazel eyes. I hoped he would inherit Mike's personality—mellow, an antidote to my not-so-mellow.

One night, a few days after we learned of the diagnosis, I dreamed that I saw our baby: he had black hair like mine, but it was long, like a hippie's, the way I'd seen Mike in yellowed black-and-white photos from the '60s. In the dream, we were in a bookstore, the three of us. I heard gunfire. Then, the baby crawled away. I woke up missing him, mourning the child we wouldn't have.

A Right to an Abortion

I'm sure pro-lifers don't give you the right to grieve for the baby you chose not to bring into the world (another euphemism, although avoiding the word "abortion" doesn't take any sting out of the decision to have one). Only now do I understand how entirely personal the decision to terminate a pregnancy is and how wrong it feels to bring someone else's morality into the discussion.

I was lucky. When I walked into the hospital, no one knew why, or cared. The nurses were kind and the doctor held my hand as the anesthesia took over.

As for that baby that will never be, I will remember him always. But I'm quite certain that I made the right choice for the three of us.

EVALUATING THE AUTHORS' ARGUMENTS:

The author of the previous viewpoint, Deborah Kendrick, has a disability herself. The author of the viewpoint you just read does not. The authors disagree about the validity of aborting a fetus with potential disabilities. Does knowing their backgrounds influence your opinion of their arguments? Why or why not?

Viewpoint

3

The Emergency Contraception Pill Is Abortion

Nathan Tabor

"The morning after pill doesn't just prevent pregnancy—it can also kill a child who has already been conceived in her mother's womb."

In the following viewpoint conservative columnist Nathan Tabor argues that the emergency contraception pill, sometimes called the morning after pill, is a dangerous medication that can cause an abortion. Despite this, women are being encouraged to get a prescription for the drug by their gynecologists, even when they do not want to. Doctors are influenced by the pro-abortion agenda of the American College of Obstetricians and Gynecologists, Tabor writes. They are endangering women's health and killing unborn children by dispensing emergency contraception.

AS YOU READ, CONSIDER THE FOLLOWING QUESTIONS:

1. What does the acronym ACOG stand for?
2. According to the author, why would big drug companies need to sell the morning after pill directly to doctors?

I magine going to your doctor and being offered a pill—not because you were sick, or in any danger of becoming sick. No—you're friendly physician is simply giving you drugs because you're a woman.

If that sounds like a Hitchcock horror story to you—be prepared. Gynecologists around the country are embarking on a weird medical experiment that could have serious repercussions for women's health.

The American College of Obstetricians and Gynecologists (ACOG) has decided it won't wait for the Food and Drug Administration to approve over-the-counter sales of the so-called morning after pill—a pill which is supposed to help women who are harboring regret over a sexual encounter the night before. Of course, it doesn't matter that the FDA is hesitant to give the pills out like candy because it doesn't want to promote promiscuity among young people. Also, some leading medical experts say that the morning after pill doesn't just prevent pregnancy—it can also kill a child who has already been conceived in her mother's womb.

> **FAST FACT**
>
> Pharmacists for Life International is an organization of pharmacists who refuse to fill prescriptions for medications they feel cause abortions.

No, ACOG won't let the facts stand in the way of its misguided idea of scientific progress. In fact, the gynecologists' group employs this fuzzy reasoning for promoting morning after pill prescriptions: women tend to have sex on weekends. Maybe women also tend to have beer on Saturday nights. Does that mean their family doctors should load them up with six packs every time they come in for flu shots?

Promoting Abortion

The fact is, the pro-abortion contingent of ACOG is running scared. Pharmacists throughout the country have said they don't want to dispense the morning after pill, also known as emergency "contra-

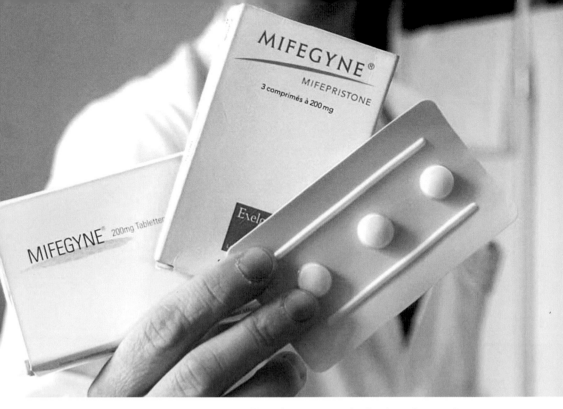

The chemicals in emergency contraception pills work to prevent a fertilized egg from implanting in the uterus, which some abortion opponents consider to be the same thing as an abortion.

ception," because they have religious and moral objections to it. The abortionists know that if they can get women hooked on the morning after pill, they'll have more support for their agenda—which includes abortion any time for any reason, anywhere.

It's interesting to note that some experts have come to the conclusion that there really isn't a great demand for the morning after pill. In other words, pharmacies are not going to go out of business for refusing to stock it. So the only way for big drug companies to sell the morning after pill and other such concoctions is to market them directly to doctors.

Pushing Emergency Contraception

Every time a woman comes into a gynecologist's office, ACOG wants the doctor to offer her advance prescriptions of the morning after pill. But it is apparently not enough to simply make the offer— some women are reporting that their gynecologists are insisting that they take the prescription—even if they say repeatedly that they don't want it. The doctors urge them, "it's good for a year!" This

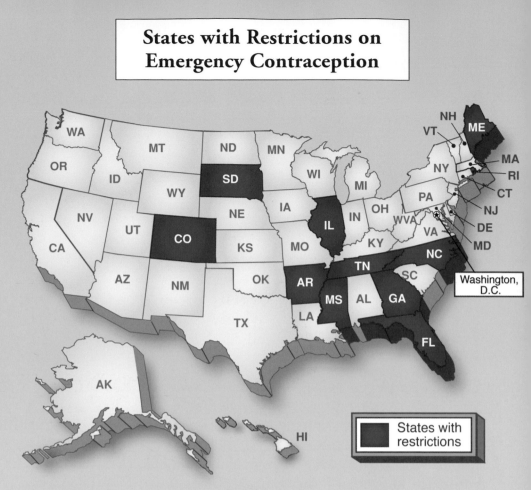

States with Restrictions on Emergency Contraception

Washington, D.C.

States with restrictions

Source: *State Policies in Brief.* Emergency Contraception, Alan Guttmacher Institute, September 1, 2006.

kind of scenario makes a mockery out of the phrase "pro-choice." In a situation like this, how can anyone not conclude that "pro-choice" is really "pro-abortion?"

Apparently, ACOG sees no reason for gynecologists to inform their patients that the morning after pill can cause abortions—even if some women have strong moral objections to abortion. For ACOG, the pill is a simple solution to the estimated 2.7 million unplanned pregnancies that occur each year.

But the fact of the matter is, a number of us were the result of unplanned pregnancies. You don't have to be planned—or even wanted by your natural parents—in order to make a difference in this world. Every human life is precious from the moment of conception—and no dictate from ACOG can change that.

Emergency Contraception Is Dangerous

Doctors routinely tell pregnant women not to take any medication during their pregnancies for fear that it will harm their unborn children. If a pregnant woman can't take an aspirin, how can doctors assume that it's safe for her to take the morning after pill? What if the pill "fails" and the woman remains pregnant? Or what if the woman takes the pill when she's already six weeks along? And what's to prevent the pill from getting into the hands of the woman's impressionable 13-year-old daughter, who sees the pill as a good excuse to "hook up" with a boy she barely knows? Will ACOG pay for the girl's counseling when she discovers that the boy who took away her virginity is a stalker or 40 years old?

Any doctor who thinks nothing of dispensing a pill that can kill has no place in the healing arts. Whether an abortion is surgical or chemical, it is still a tragedy for both mother and child.

EVALUATING THE AUTHOR'S ARGUMENTS:

All doctors take an oath swearing that they will "do no harm." Tabor accuses gynecologists of giving women prescriptions for emergency contraception, even if they do not want them. In your opinion, are these doctors violating their oath? Or are they upholding it? Give your reasons.

The Emergency Contraception Pill Is Not Abortion

Robyn E. Blumner

"[Emergency contraception] pills work primarily by delaying . . . ovulation and by inhibiting fertilization . . . there is no fertilized egg."

In the following viewpoint the author argues that medical science has proven that emergency contraceptive pills do not cause abortions and are a safe way to prevent pregnancy. The pills work by preventing fertilization of an egg. These pills should be available to women without a prescription, she writes. However, the FDA is reluctant to approve over-the-counter (OTC) status for emergency contraception because of an antiabortion political agenda. Doctors and politicians are relying on a theological definition of pregnancy, not a medical one. Robyn E. Blumner is a columnist for the *St. Petersburg Times*, a Florida newspaper.

AS YOU READ, CONSIDER THE FOLLOWING QUESTIONS:

1. How many abortions does the author estimate OTC emergency contraception can prevent?

2. What is the theory known as the "postfertilization effect"?
3. Why do some pharmacists say their faith does not allow them to provide hormonal contraceptives?

W e're waiting. The women of America, or at least the 95 percent of us who will use some form of contraception during our childbearing years, are waiting for the Food and Drug Administration [FDA] to stop putting ideology over science.

It has been nearly two years since the makers of Plan B, a morning-after emergency contraception pill, submitted an application to change the status of the two-tablet regimen from prescription-only to over-the-counter. There is only one reason the change has not been made: abortion politics. [In July 2006, the FDA approved OTC-status for Plan B for women over 18.]

At first it may seem odd that the antiabortion [George W.] Bush administration would throw up unreasonable barriers to the approval of over-the-counter emergency contraception. It is estimated

that allowing easy access to morning-after pills would prevent 1.7-million unintended pregnancies a year, including 800,000 abortions. Why wouldn't the administration jump at the chance to eliminate the need for thousands of abortions?

But dig a little deeper and a radical fringe agenda emerges. It has to do with the medical definition of pregnancy versus the theological one.

Defining Pregnancy

Emergency contraception pills are remarkably safe and highly effective at preventing pregnancy if taken within days of unprotected intercourse. The staff at the FDA and an advisory panel of experts strongly urged the agency to approve Plan B's over-the-counter availability. But last May [2004], the FDA turned down that request on the grounds that girls under 16 might have difficulty understanding

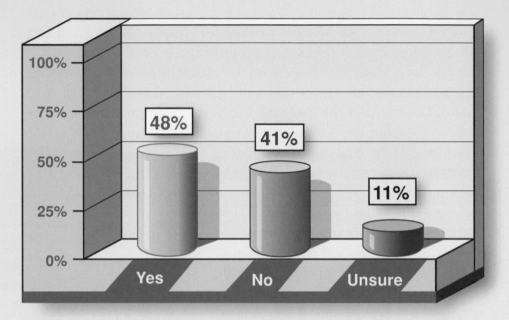

Should Emergency Contraception Be Available Without a Prescription?

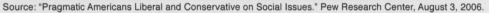

Source: "Pragmatic Americans Liberal and Conservative on Social Issues." Pew Research Center, August 3, 2006.

how to take the medication properly. (Funny, those concerns didn't stall the approval of over-the-counter sleeping aids and cough syrups.)

The pills work primarily by delaying or preventing ovulation and by inhibiting fertilization—in both these cases, there is no fertilized egg.

But there is also an unproven theory known as the "postfertilization effect" that says emergency contraception and birth control pills alike change the uterine lining in a way that prevents the egg from implanting.

This is what all the fuss is about. To a tiny minority of doctors and pharmacists and to virtually the entire Bush administration, emergency contraception is an abortifacient [a pill that causes abortion].

Pregnancy Starts at Implantation

Established medical science, however, has come to a different conclusion. The American College of Obstetricians and Gynecologists defines pregnancy as starting after a fertilized egg implants in the wall of the uterus, not the moment the egg is fertilized. Pregnancy tests won't even indicate a positive result before implantation; and it is worth noting that between 40 and 60 percent of fertilized eggs will, on their own, fail to implant. I guess that's viewed as nature's holocaust to some.

To see just how freighted the terms of the debate are, here is an exchange [in March 2005] between Sen. Hillary Rodham Clinton, D-N.Y., and Dr. Lester Crawford, acting FDA commissioner, during his confirmation hearing: "Would you clarify for the committee that emergency contraception is a method for prevention of pregnancy, not the termination of pregnancy?" Clinton asked.

Crawford responded: "I may need to confer with the experts in the FDA about exactly what the physiology of it is." He then suggested that any label would say "prevention," and then backtracked from that.

Clinton tried again to get a straight answer. She read from the FDA's own release of May 2004: "'Emergency contraception is a method of preventing pregnancy.' That is the FDA position, is that correct Dr. Crawford?"

Crawford again dissembled and obfuscated [to confuse an issue], saying he needed to "consult with the experts in the center."

He also refused, despite pointed questioning from a number of senators, to assure that Plan B would be approved as an over-the-counter drug or to say when a decision by his agency might be made.

Complicating the Issue

This obsession with a postfertilization effect is driving many of those pharmacists who are refusing to fill birth control prescriptions. They say their faith doesn't allow them in good conscience to provide hormonal contraceptives, because it might lead to a "chemical abortion" of a fertilized egg.

Before implantation, a human embryo is typically between 50 and 150 cells. Compare that to the 250,000 cells that make up the brain of a fruit fly and we can begin to see just how extreme these views are. Millions of American women may need emergency contraception in the next few years. But their ability to obtain it will be unnecessarily complicated until some semblance of common sense returns to Washington.

EVALUATING THE AUTHORS' ARGUMENTS:

In the viewpoint you just read, Robyn E. Blumner argues that emergency contraception is not an abortifacient—a pill that causes abortion. In the previous viewpoint, Nathan Tabor disagrees. Emergency contraception kills an unborn child, he says. Both authors cite medical science to support their points. With which argument do you agree? Using evidence from the viewpoints, state your reasons.

Late-Term Abortions Should Be Banned

Antony Barone Kolenc

"Without the ban, the medical profession is on a slippery slope that makes it more acceptable to devalue human life."

Antony Barone Kolenc is a professor of constitutional law at the U.S. Air Force Academy. In the following viewpoint he argues that Congress was right to ban late-term abortion, also called partial-birth abortion, because the process is cruel and inhumane. In 2000 the Supreme Court struck down a state ban on the procedure, calling it unconstitutional, but despite this, Congress passed a federal ban on late-term abortions, Kolenc writes. Though the ban is sure to be overturned later, it has been useful nonetheless because it has focused public attention on this important issue. Late-term abortion must not be permitted, Kolenc states.

AS YOU READ, CONSIDER THE FOLLOWING QUESTIONS:

1. In what year did the public first become aware of partial-birth abortion?
2. What is the name of the 2000 Supreme Court decision striking down Nebraska's abortion ban?

Antony Barone Kolenc, "Legal Failure or Moral Success?" *America*, vol. 191, November 29, 2004, pp. 11–14, © America Press Inc., 2004. All rights reserved. www.americamagazine.org. Reproduced with permission of America Press, Inc., 106 West 56th Street, New York, NY 10019.

3. The author gives two key reasons partial-birth abortion should be banned. Name one of these.

Does the ban on partial-birth abortion really save babies' lives? Does the ban violate the U.S. Constitution? How crucial is the ban to the pro-life movement? [In the summer of 2004], federal judges in California, New York and Nebraska dealt a major setback to pro-life efforts to ban the controversial partial-birth abortion procedure. The judges found that the ban violates the U.S. Constitution. The ban on partial-birth abortion has become a victim of risky political strategies and legal failures. Yet, despite its flaws, the ban has posted strong successes for the pro-life movement by molding public opinion and raising awareness about the evils of abortion.

Awareness of the Procedure

Partial-birth abortion came to public attention in 1992 during a presentation given by Marvin Haskell, M.D., to the National Abortion Federation. Some doctors claim to have performed similar techniques since the 1970's. When the American public discovered the facts about partial-birth abortion, many united to speak on behalf of the unborn. A political movement took shape to ban the procedure. The issue became the new rallying cry for the pro-life movement.

Overnight, the procedure was tagged as the most inhumane method of abortion, causing severe pain to an unborn child who is already in the process of a live birth. The method is commonly compared to infanticide, because the child is almost entirely delivered before the abortion doctor brutally ends his or her life. This is done by crushing the child's skull just moments before the first breath. . . .

> **FAST FACT**
>
> In 2000 South Dakota became the first state to ban late-term abortions entirely.

Ban Unconstitutional

By the end of the 1990's, many Christians and other pro-life activists rejoiced that 30 states had banned the cruel procedure, but their victory celebration was short-lived. In *Stenberg v. Carhart*, a Supreme Court decision in 2000, a sharply divided court struck down Nebraska's partial-birth abortion ban as a violation of the U.S. Constitution. The court decided that the ban was too broad and might place an "undue burden" on a woman's ability to choose other "legal" methods of abortion. It also struck down the ban because it did not contain a "health exception." This exception would allow doctors to perform partial-birth abortions when it was "safer" for the mother's health.

The dissenting Supreme Court justices criticized the court's new "health exception," because it would make the ban meaningless. If abortion doctors determine when the procedure is "necessary," then, they reasoned, no state could ever realistically enforce the ban.

Congress Passes a Defiant Federal Ban

Before *Stenberg*, Congress had joined the states in passing a federal partial-birth abortion ban. But President [Bill] Clinton had vetoed

Right to Life of Michigan president Barbara Listing greets the media at a press conference in 2004. The boxes behind her contain petitions to outlaw partial-birth abortions in Michigan.

it many times because it did not include a "health exception." With the election of George W. Bush in 2000, new hope rose that a federal ban could be achieved.

Guided by *Stenberg*, Congress rewrote its ban so that it would not apply to other "legal" methods of abortion. This had been a major defect, according to the court, in the unconstitutional Nebraska law. But Congress refused to add a "health exception" to the law. Instead, Congress took a gamble on a risky political strategy that pitted it directly against the Supreme Court.

After conducting numerous hearings, Congress concluded that the partial-birth abortion procedure was never medically necessary to preserve a mother's health; in fact, it found that the procedure posed serious health risks to the mother. With these conclusions in hand, Congress defied the Supreme Court and passed a ban on partial-birth abortion that did not contain the "health exception" required by *Stenberg*.

Signed into Law

On Nov. 5, 2003, President Bush signed the federal partial-birth abortion ban, stating: "For years, a terrible form of violence has been directed against children who are inches from birth, while the law looked the other way. Today, at last, the American people and our government have confronted the violence and come to the defense of the innocent child."

Less than a year later three federal courts ruled that the ban is unconstitutional. Congress's risky strategy has turned into a tragic legal failure. The judges who recently struck down the ban did not give Congress the deference that its findings of fact had traditionally received. Instead, they viewed Congress's findings as self-contradictory and partially false. As a result, the partial-birth abortion ban is now in jeopardy.

Reasons to Support the Ban

Supporters of the ban on partial-birth abortion have asserted two key reasons for banning the horrid procedure. First, they argue that the law prohibits a procedure that is more akin to infanticide than abortion. In his dissent from the *Stenberg* decision, Justice Anthony Kennedy explained why the ban is necessary. He wrote: "States also

States with Late-Term Abortion Bans

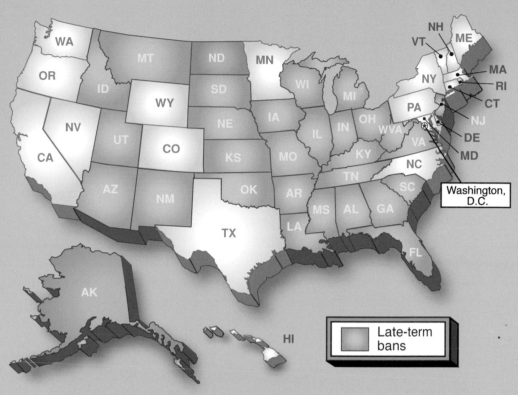

Source: Center for Reproductive Rights, February 22, 2006.

have an interest in forbidding medical procedures which . . . cause the medical profession or society as a whole to become insensitive, even disdainful, to life. . . ." Partial-birth abortion is different from other abortion methods because "the fetus is 'killed outside of the womb' where the fetus has an autonomy which separates it from the right of the woman to choose treatments for her own body."

Without the ban, the medical profession is on a slippery slope that makes it more acceptable to devalue human life and kill even those babies who are just inches from birth.

Pro-life activists also point to a second reason why the ban is so crucial. Experts have testified that partial-birth abortion causes "prolonged and excruciating pain" to unborn children. Studies have shown that during the middle stages of fetal growth an unborn child has a deeper sense of pain than the child will have after birth. Thus, the ban can spare innocent children the prolonged and severe pain associated with the procedure. . . .

Abortion Education Is Important

The partial-birth abortion ban is not perfect and provides only slight protection for unborn children. Yet despite its deficiency, the ban has succeeded in educating society and in swaying public opinion to help the unborn. The partial-birth abortion issue has kept the abortion debate at the forefront of the American conversation. . . .

People should support truthful education about abortion and its gruesome methods. As the partial-birth abortion issue has demonstrated, when the American public is informed about the evils of abortion, it will respond appropriately and demand action.

When the vast majority of Americans see the unborn child as a person and a victim, when the average American understands abortion to be a cruel and gruesome procedure, then the fruit of the labors to ban partial-birth abortion may be harvested. Until then, the fight continues.

EVALUATING THE AUTHORS' ARGUMENTS:

In the viewpoint you just read, Antony Barone Kolenc refers to the procedure under discussion as "partial-birth abortion," a phrase commonly used by pro-life supporters. In the next viewpoint, Gretchen Voss calls the same procedure "late-term abortion," the phrase usually used by pro-choice advocates. What effect are the authors trying to achieve with their choice of language? Which term do you prefer? Why?

Late-Term Abortions Should Be Available

"We both knew what we needed to do. . . . We decided to terminate the pregnancy. It was our last parental decision."

Gretchen Voss

In the following viewpoint author Gretchen Voss argues that late-term abortion is a necessary procedure that must be available for both the health of the mother and for fetuses with profound birth defects. She states that the congressional ban on the procedure uses faulty science and provocative language to distort the issue. Using her own late-term abortion experience to illustrate the difficulty of such a decision, Voss writes that the real experiences of women have become lost in political ideology. When the viewpoint begins, Voss is describing learning that her baby has severe birth defects.

AS YOU READ, CONSIDER THE FOLLOWING QUESTIONS:

1. What are the names of the two procedures that are prohibited under the congressional late-term abortion ban, according to the author?

2. What is a reason named in the viewpoint that a mother might have an abortion?

Gretchen Voss, "My Late-Term Abortion," *Boston Globe Magazine*, January 25, 2004. Reproduced by permission of the author.

3. Why do legal scholars think the federal late-term abortion ban will be ruled unconstitutional?

Instead of cinnamon and spice, our child came with technical terms like hydrocephalus and spina bifida. The spine, [the doctor] said, had not closed properly, and because of the location of the opening, it was as bad as it got. What they knew—that the baby would certainly be paralyzed and incontinent, that the baby's brain was being tugged against the opening in the base of the skull and the cranium was full of fluid—was awful. What they didn't know—whether the baby would live at all, and if so, with what sort of mental and developmental defects—was devastating. Countless surgeries would be required if the baby did live. None of them would repair the damage that was already done.

We met with a genetic counselor, but given the known as well as the unknown, we both knew what we needed to do. Though the baby might live, it was not a life that we would choose for our child, a child that we already loved. We decided to terminate the pregnancy. It was our last parental decision.

So this is our story—mine, my husband's, and our baby's. It's not a story I ever thought I'd share with a mass audience, because, frankly, it's nobody's business. But now it is.

FAST FACT

There are only five hundred to six hundred late-term abortions performed per year in the United States.

Late-Term Abortion Banned

On November 5 [2003], George W. Bush signed the first federal ban on any abortion procedure in the 30 years since *Roe v. Wade*, and the first ban of a surgical technique in the history of this country. . . .

At the heart of the debate is a term that legislators concocted. They created a nonexistent procedure—partial-birth abortion—and then banned it. They then gave it such a purposely vague definition that, according to abortion providers as well as the Supreme Court, which ruled a similar law in Nebraska unconstitutional, it could apply to all abortions after the first trimester.

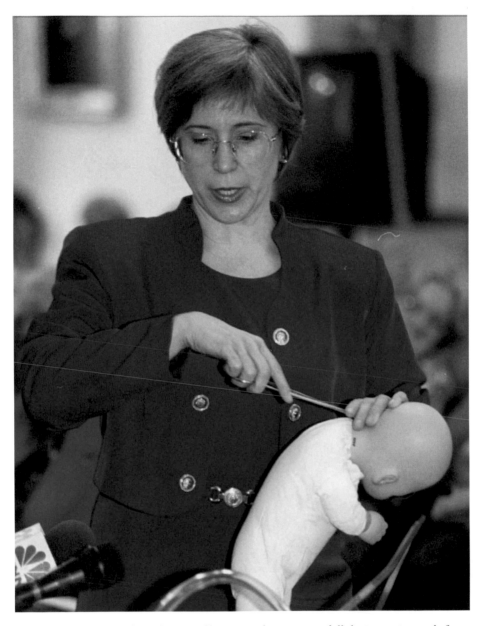

A doctor demonstrates the technique of late-term abortion on a doll during testimony before a Vermont legislative committee considering a ban on the procedure.

Though some proponents of the bill say that they merely want to ban a specific medical procedure—properly called intact dilation and extraction, which accounts for fewer than one-fifth of 1 percent of all abortions in this country, according to a 2000 survey by the Alan Guttmacher Institute—they never specifically called it that.

Instead, the bill is written in such a way that the much more common procedure—dilation and evacuation, which accounts for 96 percent of second-trimester abortions, including my own—would also be banned. . . .

Serious Consequences

So what does it all really mean? It means that all abortions after the first trimester could be outlawed. No matter if the fetus has severe birth defects, including those incompatible with life (many of which cannot be detected until well into the second trimester). No matter if the mother would be forced to have, for example, a kidney transplant or a hysterectomy if she continued with the pregnancy. Legislators did not provide a health exception for the woman, arguing that it would provide too big a loophole. In the aftermath of the signing of the bill, its supporters spoke about having outlawed a medical procedure and protecting the nation's children. "We have

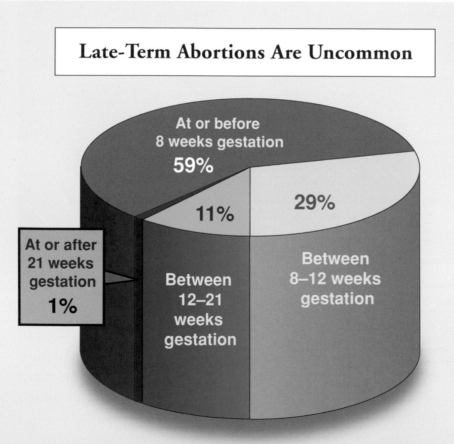

Late-Term Abortions Are Uncommon

At or before 8 weeks gestation **59%**

11%

29%

At or after 21 weeks gestation **1%**

Between 12–21 weeks gestation

Between 8–12 weeks gestation

Source: "Abortion in Women's Lives," Alan Guttmacher Institute, May 2006.

just outlawed a procedure that is barbaric, that is brutal, that is offensive to our moral sensibilities," said Bill Frist, the Senate majority leader [at the time].

Its opponents bemoaned an unconstitutional attack on legal rights. "This ban is yet another instance of the federal government inappropriately interfering in the private lives of Americans, dangerously undermining . . . the very foundation of a woman's right to privacy," said Gregory T. Nojeim, an associate director and chief legislative counsel for the American Civil Liberties Union.

But lost in the political slugfest have been the very real experiences of women—and their families—who face this heartbreaking decision every day. . . .

Ideology vs. Reality

I don't remember much from those three days. Walking around with a belly full of broken dreams, it felt like what I would imagine drowning feels like—flailing and suffocating and desperate. Semiconscious. Surrounded by our family, I found myself tortured by our decision, asking over and over, are we doing the right thing? That was the hardest part. Even though I finally understood that pregnancy wasn't a Gerber commercial, that bringing forth life was intimately wrapped up in death—what with miscarriage and stillbirth—this was actually a choice. Everyone said, of course it's the right thing to do—even my Catholic father and my Republican father-in-law, neither of whom was ever "pro-choice." Because suddenly, for them, it wasn't about religious doctrine or political platforms. It was personal—their son, their daughter, their grandchild. It was flesh and blood, as opposed to abstract ideology, and that changed everything. . . .

Federal and State Bans Unconstitutional

The trio of lawsuits that has been filed points to the Supreme Court's decision [in 2003] that overturned a similar so-called partial-birth abortion ban in Nebraska. The court, in *Stenberg v. Carhart*, ruled in a narrow, 5-4 decision that the ban was unconstitutional on two grounds: the lack of an exception to protect a woman's health; and the fact that the ban would prohibit even the most commonly used and medically safe abortion procedures throughout the second trimester of pregnancy. Many legal scholars think that this federal ban will also be ruled unconstitutional on those same grounds. . . .

Leaving Women Without Choices

The doctor who performed my termination talks about the women he has helped through the years—the pregnant woman who was diagnosed with metastatic melanoma and needed immediate chemotherapy, the woman who was carrying conjoined twins that had only one set of lungs and one heart, the woman whose baby had a three-chambered heart and would never live. Now, he is turning these women away. "Now, today, I can say no, but what is she going to do?" he says sadly. "What is she going to do?". . .

As . . . prenatal testing results [for our second pregnancy] started to pile up, all of them completely normal, we began to let hope back into our hearts. Of course, we know that anything can happen at any time. We'll never forget that. There will be many more months of worry— and then, I guess, a lifetime more. At least for now, though, things look hopeful for our son. But I worry about my friends who are planning to have children now and in the near future, friends who are as naive as I once was. It's a different world these days. "Now, it's like the Stone Age, it's like a Muslim country here," says the doctor who performed my procedure. "This is the most backward law, it is not for a civilized country. If this was Iran, Iraq, I wouldn't be surprised. But to pass this law in the United States, what is this government doing?"

EVALUATING THE AUTHOR'S ARGUMENTS:

In the Voss viewpoint, a doctor is quoted as saying that the congressional late-term abortion ban "is the most backward law, it is not for a civilized country." *Civilized* means having an advanced, humane culture. Using this definition, do you agree or disagree with the doctor's statement? Does the ban make the United States a more or less "civilized" nation?

Chapter 3

Who Controls Abortion Decisions?

IT'S YOUR CHOI
...NOT THEIRS.

i ♥ pro-choice
boys

CHOOSE
JUSTICE

One issue in the abortion debate is whether or not men should have any say in abortion decisions.

Parental Consent Is Necessary for Teenage Abortions

Clarke D. Forsythe

"[Minors] need the guidance of parents to assess the risks of abortion."

Clarke D. Forsythe is an attorney who works for the Americans United for Life, a pro-life organization in Chicago. In the following viewpoint he states that the Supreme Court should uphold a New Hampshire law that requires parents to give consent before a minor can have an abortion. The law has an exception for true medical emergencies, but Planned Parenthood has brought the suit because it believes the law needs to have an exception for health, rather than just medical emergencies. The Court has been vague about how to define health exceptions in the past, Forsythe writes, leaving the definition open to almost any sort of distress. In order to protect teenagers, the Court must define the health exception of the law narrowly, he argues.

AS YOU READ, CONSIDER THE FOLLOWING QUESTIONS:

1. What is one reason given by the author that parents should be notified before minor girls have an abortion?
2. What is the difference between a health exception and a medical emergency exception, according to Forsythe?
3. What action does the author believe the Court should take regarding the health exception?

An overwhelming majority of Americans (70–80 percent) support notifying parents before an abortion on a minor girl, and for good reason. Minors are usually too immature to assess the safety of abortion clinics, the alternatives to abortion, or to recall their own medical history. In addition, they need the guidance of parents to assess the risks of abortion—like increased risk of placenta previa [an obstetrical complication] and premature births in future pregnancies, increased alcohol and drug abuse after abortion, or the increased risk of suicide after abortion.

FAST FACT

Of all the states requiring parental consent for an abortion, only Idaho does not allow for a judicial bypass.

And parental notice is necessary to enable parents to care for their daughter afterwards. If parents don't know what their daughter has been through, how can they check for any signs of extensive bleeding, fever, infection, or psychological distress? Even if there's a life-threatening medical emergency, parents need to be notified, if only after the emergency subsides.

Parental-Notice Laws Are Necessary

For these reasons, the Supreme Court has repeatedly approved parental-notice laws—at least rhetorically—since 1981. While half the states have parental-notice or consent laws, half have no laws in place, including New Hampshire. Most laws are passed only to be bottled up for years in litigation filed by Planned Parenthood or abortion clinics.

[On November 30, 2005], the Supreme Court will hear arguments in *Ayotte v. Planned Parenthood* about the validity of the New Hampshire parental notice of abortion law, which a federal appeals-court decision struck down [in 2004].

There are two major questions in this case. First, will the Court uphold the law and allow parents to have notification in New Hampshire? Second, will the Court recognize the mess it has created with its vague and contradictory decisions and clarify the standards for federal courts to assess critical requirements like parental notice?

Exception for Health of Mother

New Hampshire patterned its law after the Minnesota parental-notice law which has been in effect for nearly 20 years with a positive impact on reducing adolescent pregnancy, birth, and abortion rates. The Supreme Court upheld the Minnesota law in 1990.

The New Hampshire law (copying the Minnesota law) has a narrowly drafted exception for real, life-threatening medical emergencies. The general rule for medical treatment is that parents must give consent (not just notice) before a doctor can treat any minor child, unless there is a life-threatening medical emergency. While some state legislatures have adopted exceptions to this general rule over the past decades—for prenatal care, sexually transmitted disease, and drug addiction—the exceptions are relatively narrow.

Planned Parenthood challenged the New Hampshire law because Planned Parenthood insists that parental-notice and consent laws in every state must have a "health" exception rather than a "medical emergency" exception.

A Vague Definition

But the Supreme Court has created its own unique and unlimited definition of "health" in abortion law, defining "health" as "all factors —physical, emotional, psychological, familial, and the woman's age—relevant to the well-being of the patient." "Health" means emotional well-being without limits. Thus, a "health" exception in abortion law is virtually the opposite of a real "medical emergency."

States Requiring Parental Involvement in Minors' Abortions

Required
Not required

Source: "Parental Involvement in Minors' Abortions." *State Policies in Brief*, Alan Guttmacher Institute, September 1, 2006.

Any potential emotional reservation a minor girl might have about a pregnancy (including pressure to have the abortion from her 22-year-old "boyfriend") would be a "health" reason for the abortion without parental notice. Since this unlimited "health exception" would swallow the requirement of parental notice, the Supreme Court should reject the "health" exception and uphold the New Hampshire medical emergency exception. . . .

The Court could—and may—uphold the New Hampshire parental-notice law without addressing or resolving the confusion that it has created. The Court is long overdue to correct this situation, but, there's no guarantee the Court will fix the mess in *Ayotte*.

EVALUATING THE AUTHOR'S ARGUMENTS:

In the viewpoint you just read, the author argues that doctors could perform an abortion without first notifying parents only in the case of a life-threatening medical emergency. Planned Parenthood believes that doctors should be allowed to perform an abortion without parental notification if there is a threat to a girl's health, even if it is not life threatening, such as a risk to her future fertility. With which argument do you agree? Give your reasons.

Viewpoint

2

"If the Supreme Court accepts the arguments put forth . . . , it could effectively eliminate the requirement that abortion laws must include protections for women's health."

Parental Consent Is Unnecessary for Teenage Abortions

Joan Malin

In the following viewpoint the president of Planned Parenthood of New York City, Joan Malin, argues that the Supreme Court must strike down the New Hampshire law being considered in *Ayotte v. Planned Parenthood*. The law places women and girls who need an abortion to protect their health in grave danger. In addition it undermines *Roe v. Wade*, which gave every woman the right to an abortion. Doctors must be able to treat sick pregnant girls and women without the courts' interference, even if that means providing an abortion.

AS YOU READ, CONSIDER THE FOLLOWING QUESTIONS:

1. What are two of the conditions pregnant women in medical crisis can suffer, according to the author?
2. Summarize the two issues being decided in the Supreme Court case.

Abortion, abortion, abortion. Aren't you tired of hearing about abortion rights? And now [in the] Supreme Court case *Ayotte v. Planned Parenthood of Northern New England et al*—it's all over the news again. Isn't it enough already?

No, it's not. Because this case, *Ayotte v. Planned Parenthood of Northern New England et al*, is bringing us to the brink of the previously unimaginable: pregnant women in severe medical crisis unable to seek relief or protection until they have already suffered grave physical damage, such as liver or kidney dysfunction, infertility, diabetes, or chronic pain.

No Health Protection

Ayotte v. Planned Parenthood of Northern New England et al began as a case challenging a New Hampshire law that prevents doctors from performing an abortion for a teenager under the age of 18 until 48 hours after a parent has been notified. Contrary, however, to 30 years of Supreme Court precedent, the law contains no medical emergency exception to protect a pregnant teenager's health. Two federal courts have already struck down the law as unconstitutional because of this omission. There are two issues now being decided in this case and the stakes are immense.

FAST FACT

A pregnant woman or girl's kidneys and liver can sustain major damage if medical care is delayed during pregnancy complications.

First, the case asks if abortion restrictions must include medical emergency exceptions to protect a woman's health. When it comes to women's health, the Supreme Court has been clear: for 30 years, the court has consistently held that abortion laws must include protections for women's health. When a woman is facing a medical emergency, her doctor must be able to provide urgently needed care—not have his or her hands tied by an anti-abortion law that requires a delay in treating the patient. A doctor's top priority is always the health and safety of his or her patients; doctors, not judges, should make decisions in medical emergencies.

The New Hampshire attorney general and the Bush administration, however, are asking those health-saving protections be removed. If the Supreme Court accepts the arguments put forth by the New Hampshire attorney general and the Bush administration, it could effectively eliminate the requirement that abortion laws must include protections for women's health, potentially affecting laws in all fifty states.

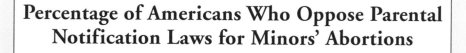

Percentage of Americans Who Oppose Parental Notification Laws for Minors' Abortions

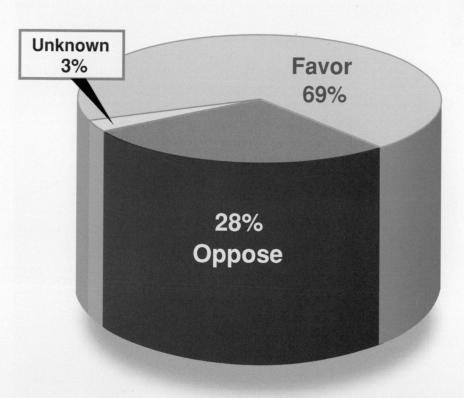

Source: Gallup Poll, November 11–13, 2005.

A clinic intake worker waits for paperwork from a teenage client. Some abortion supporters feel that teenagers should have the same privacy rights as adults when seeking an abortion.

Arguing for a New Legal Standard

The second question is what legal test courts must use to decide whether to strike down a law that harms women. Under the existing legal standard, courts can strike down dangerous abortion restrictions before they go into effect if the restrictions place a substantial obstacle in the path of women seeking abortions.

The New Hampshire attorney general and the Bush administration are arguing for a new legal standard that would take away the ability to stop dangerous antiabortion laws even when doctors believe the laws would harm women's health. Incredibly, the government is arguing that courts should require doctors to wait until their patients risk immediate harm before coming to a court and challenging a dangerous restriction.

Undermining *Roe*

By agreeing to argue this case along with New Hampshire, the Bush administration is making another attempt to chip away at the *Roe v. Wade* decision that made abortion legal nationwide.

Chillingly, while *Roe* has not been overturned, nearly as alarming is the slow and steady dismantling of reproductive freedoms by state legislatures and the federal government. When the Supreme Court decided *Planned Parenthood of Southeastern Pennsylvania v. Casey* in 1992 [the Casey case decision upheld a state law that restricted abortion], it unlocked the door to hundreds of state and federal criminal restrictions designed to discourage and/or prevent women from accessing abortion services. Of the nearly 400 abortion restrictions enacted since 1992, none would have been constitutional under the original *Roe* decision.

Right to Choose Diminished

Our country is, with tragic implications, approaching an environment where abortion restrictions may not harm a wealthy woman in an anti-choice state who could afford to fly to New York, Chicago or Los Angeles for an abortion. But unfortunately, low-income women may face the non-choice of a dangerous, illegal procedure or a forced pregnancy. A woman's inherent right to decide what's best for herself, her family and her health should not be held hostage to the misfortune of geography and financial wherewithal.

The Supreme Court and state legislatures hold women's health and lives in their hands. We hope that what emerges is not a nation in which the right to choose abortion remains technically legal yet crippled by burdensome restrictions that render it inaccessible to most and unsafe for all.

EVALUATING THE AUTHORS' ARGUMENTS:

The case of *Ayotte v. Planned Parenthood* centers around a law requiring parents to be notified before a teenager has an abortion. The author of the previous viewpoint, Clarke D. Forsythe, believes teenagers are too immature to assess whether or not an abortion is necessary, even if notifying parents would threaten a girl's health. The author of the viewpoint you just read, Joan Malin, states that the law places pregnant teenagers' health in danger. Do you think that teenagers should be allowed to decide for themselves whether or not to have an abortion? Why or why not?

Men Should Have Abortion Rights Also

Meghan Daum

"Why shouldn't men have the right . . . to terminate their legal and financial rights and responsibilities to the [unborn] child?"

In 2005 Supreme Court nominee Samuel Alito stated that he believed wives should obtain their husbands' consent before having abortions. In the following viewpoint *Los Angeles Times* columnist Meghan Daum argues that while she does not agree with this idea specifically, she does believe that men should have some choice with regard to the fetuses they helped create. Men should have the option to terminate their legal and financial rights to an unborn child if their pregnant partner refuses to have an abortion, Daum writes. Just as women have a range of options such as abortion or adoption, men should have similar choices.

AS YOU READ, CONSIDER THE FOLLOWING QUESTIONS:

1. What is one problem that Daum acknowledges with Dalton Conley's argument?

2. What are two groups that would disagree with Daum's argument, according to her?

3. What is one problem that Daum acknowledges with her own argument?

For pro-choicers like myself, Supreme Court nominee Samuel A. Alito Jr.'s position regarding spousal consent for abortion seems like one more loose rock in the ongoing erosion of *Roe vs. Wade*. Even those of us who are too young to remember the pre-*Roe* era often see any threat to abortion rights as a threat to our very destinies. We are, after all, the generation that grew up under Title IX, singing along to "Free to Be You and Me" (you know, the 1972 children's record where Marlo Thomas and Alan Alda remind us that mommies can be plumbers and boys can have dolls). When it comes to self-determination, we're as determined as it gets.

But even though I was raised believing in the inviolability of a woman's right to choose, the older I get, the more I wonder if this idea of choice is being fairly applied.

Most people now accept that women, especially teenagers, often make decisions regarding abortion based on educational and career goals and whether the father of the unborn child is someone they want to hang around with for the next few decades. The "choice" in this equation is not only a matter of whether to carry an individual fetus to term but a question of what kind of life the woman wishes to lead.

Men Should Have Abortion Rights

But what about the kind of life men want to lead? On Dec. 1 [2005], Dalton Conley, director of the Center for Advanced Social Science Research at New York University, published an article on the Op-Ed page of the *New York Times* arguing that Alito's position on spousal consent did not go far enough.

Describing his own experience with a girlfriend who terminated a pregnancy against his wishes, Conley took some brave steps down the slippery slope of this debate, suggesting that if a father is willing to assume full responsibility for a child not wanted by a mother, he should be able to obtain an injunction stopping her from having an abortion—and he should be able to do so regardless of whether or not he's married to her.

Congressman Charles Canady stands next to an abortion poster during a Capitol Hill news conference in 1995 after the House passed a bill to ban a specific kind of late-term abortion.

Conley freely acknowledges the many obvious caveats in this position—the most salient being the fact that regardless of how "full" that male responsibility might be, the physical burden of pregnancy and childbirth will always put most of the onus on women. But as much as I shudder at the idea of a man, husband or not, obtaining an injunction telling me what I can or cannot do with my own body, I would argue that it is Conley who has not gone far enough.

Men Need Right to Protect Own Futures

Since we're throwing around radical ideas about abortion rights, let me raise this question: If abortion is to remain legal and relatively unrestricted—and I believe it should—why shouldn't men have the right during at least the first trimester of pregnancy to terminate their legal and financial rights and responsibilities to the child?

As Conley laments, the law does not currently allow for men to protect the futures of the fetuses they help create. What he doesn't mention—indeed, no one ever seems to—is the degree to which men also cannot protect their own futures. The way the law is now, a man who gets a woman pregnant is not only powerless to force her to terminate the pregnancy, he also has a complete legal obligation to support that child for at least 18 years.

In other words, although women are able to take control of their futures by choosing from at least a small range of options—abortion, adoption or keeping the child—a man can be forced to be a father to a child he never wanted and cannot financially support. I even know of cases in which the woman absolves the man of responsibility, only to have the courts demand payment anyway. That takes the notion of "choice" very far from anything resembling equality.

A Problematic Theory

I realize I've just alienated feminists (among whose ranks I generally count myself) as well as pro-lifers, neither of whom are always above platitudes such as "You should have kept your pants on." But that reasoning is by now as reductive as suggesting that a rape victim "asked for it." Yes, people often act irresponsibly and yes, abortion should be avoided whenever possible. But just as women should not be punished for choosing to terminate a pregnancy, men should not be punished when those women choose not to.

One problem, of course, is that the child is likely to bear the brunt of whatever punishment remains to be doled out. A father who terminates his rights, although not technically a deadbeat dad, has still helped create a kid who is not fully supported. And (in case you were wondering) there are dozens of other holes in my theory as well: What if a husband wants to terminate his rights—should that be allowed? What if a father is underage and wants to terminate but his parents forbid him? Should a father's decision-making time be limited to the first trimester? Should couples on first dates discuss their positions on the matter? Should Internet dating profiles let men check a box saying "will waive parental rights" next to the box indicating his astrological sign?

Broader Definition of Choice

There's also the danger that my idea is not just a slippery slope but a major mudslide on the way to Conley's idea. If a man can legally dissociate himself from a pregnancy, some will argue, why couldn't he also bind himself to it and force it to term? That notion horrifies me, just as my plan probably horrifies others. But that doesn't mean these ideas aren't worth discussing. Though it may be hard to find an adult male who's sufficiently undiplomatic to admit out loud that he'd like to have the option I'm proposing, let alone potentially take it, I know more than a few parents of teenage boys who lose sleep over the prospect of their sons landing in the kind of trouble from which they'll have no power to extricate themselves.

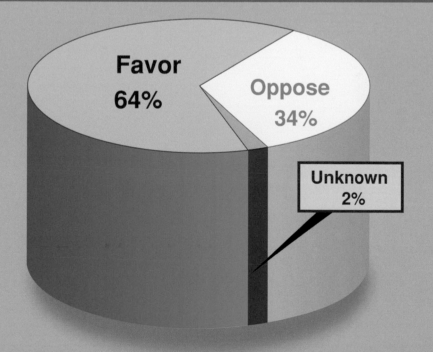

A Majority of Americans Favor a Law Requiring Husbands to Be Notified Before Wives' Abortions

Do you favor or oppose the following proposal . . . a law requiring that the husband of a married woman be notified if she decides to have an abortion?

Favor
64%

Oppose
34%

Unknown
2%

Source: CNN / *USA Today* / Gallup Poll, November 11–13, 2005.

And although the notion of women "tricking" men into fatherhood now sounds arcane and sexist, we'd be blind not to recognize the extent to which some women are capable of tricking themselves into thinking men will stick around, despite all evidence to the contrary. Allowing men to legally (if not always gracefully) bow out of fatherhood would, at the very least, start a conversation for which we haven't yet found the right words.

Actually, there's one word we've had all along: choice. We just need to broaden its definition.

EVALUATING THE AUTHOR'S ARGUMENTS:

Meghan Daum points out that it takes both a man and a woman to make a baby. Yet while women can decide what to do with their fetuses, men have no choice. Based on this knowledge, do you think that men should have the right to make abortion decisions?

Men Should Not Have Abortion Rights

Kim Gandy

> *"Some men are saying they should have 'reproductive choices' too. . . . It's absurd."*

Kim Gandy is the president of NOW, the National Organization for Women, a women's rights lobbying group. In the following viewpoint she discusses a lawsuit recently filed by a man saying that because his girlfriend refused to have an abortion, he should not have to pay child support. Gandy disagrees with this idea, stating that men should not be allowed to terminate their rights to an unborn child if they do not want it or to force women to give birth if they do. Both decisions threaten a woman's bodily integrity, Gandy writes, and take away her right to choose protected by *Roe v. Wade*.

AS YOU READ, CONSIDER THE FOLLOWING QUESTIONS:

1. Summarize Matt Dubay's argument in his case against his ex-girlfriend.
2. Why does the National Center for Men believe women should sign a reproductive rights affidavit before sexual intercourse?

3. What does Gandy say that reproductive choice for men would mean in reality?

The good news . . . that more and more men are sharing duties on the home front. The bad news is that groups claiming to represent fathers are really out to restrict women's options.

With . . . an anti-abortion rights battle spreading from state to state, I was encouraged to hear . . . that the National Center for Men planned to join the fight for reproductive rights. It's always good to have friends in battle, right?

Until I heard the rest of the story: It's their own "rights" they're concerned about.

Father's Rights

You probably heard about this so-called "father's rights" lawsuit, even though the resulting media outcry was over as quick as it began. The National Center for Men is still pushing ahead, though: The suit was filed on March 9 [2006] in U.S. District Court, on behalf of Matt Dubay, the 25-year-old Michigan man who is suing his ex-girlfriend to avoid paying child support for their infant daughter.

Dubay's logic? Well, she could have had an abortion. That was her choice. He ought to have a "choice" too, and since he didn't, he shouldn't have to help support the child.

> **FAST FACT**
>
> The number of people favoring a law requiring the husband of a married woman to be notified before she has an abortion dropped from 72 percent in 2003 to 64 percent in 2005, according to a CNN/*USA Today*/Gallup poll.

It's ironic, isn't it? The threat of women losing our bodily integrity grows larger with every passing day, with politicians telling us that our most personal decisions should be theirs to make. And now some men are saying they should have "reproductive choices" too—in other words, if he wants a baby, he should be able to force her to give birth, and if he doesn't want any responsibility, then he should be able to force her to have an abortion. It's absurd.

Women Can Be Forced to Have a Baby

In some of the media interviews I saw with the National Center for Men, they even argued that women should be asked to sign a "reproductive rights affidavit" before engaging in intercourse with men. I can only imagine how that conversation would start: "Just so we're clear. . ." My advice to any woman who is presented with one of these 'affidavits': Run!

These men go so far as to say, "Only women have the extraordinary freedom to enjoy sexual intimacy free from the fear of forced parenthood." Did I hear that right? Only a person who had never had sleepless nights fearing an unplanned pregnancy, never had to rush to the drug store for emergency contraception after a broken condom or, much worse, a sexual assault, would make such a ridiculous statement. The lawsuit reads, in part, "I will challenge any court order that seeks to impose a parental obligation upon me against my will. . . ."

"Imposing parental obligation," hmm? As in, forcing a woman to have a baby she doesn't want and can't provide for? No, they're not concerned with that.

Women's eNews 5/6/04 ANNTELNAES

Men Need to Take Responsibility

According to the National Center for Men Web site, as a result of *Roe v. Wade*, "[w]omen now have control of their lives after an unplanned conception. But men are routinely forced to give up control, forced to be financially responsible for choices only women are permitted to make, forced to relinquish reproductive choice as the price of intimacy." That's a whole lot of talk that, when you get right down to it, means "have an abortion or I get to walk away." Either way it means zero consequences and zero responsibility, and they want the courts to call it "reproductive choice for men."

And no choice for women at all.

EVALUATING THE AUTHORS' ARGUMENTS:

The authors of the preceding viewpoints, Kim Gandy and Meghan Daum, agree that there are potential dangers in permitting fathers to make decisions about abortions. What are some of the dangers they name? Does taking these into account influence your opinion on whether or not fathers should have abortion rights? Why or why not?

Facts About Abortion

Abortion Past and Present

- Medieval Europeans recorded recipes for abortion-inducing medicines that included willow, Queen Anne's lace, hawthorn, and pennyroyal.
- Folk methods for inducing abortion are myriad and include having a woman sneeze, jump about, drink alcohol, take hot baths, or douche with urine.
- Abortion was the leading cause of maternal mortality in the years before it was legalized.
- The procedure commonly known as partial-birth abortion is called intact dilation and extraction, or D&X, by the medical establishment.
- Prenatal testing can detect up to 450 conditions that can cause birth defects in the fetus.
- The average cost of a first-trimester abortion is around $350.
- Women who are young, poor, black, and unmarried are most likely to experience a delay when seeking an abortion.

Abortion in the United States

- Approximately 30 million American women have had abortions since the passage of *Roe v. Wade* in 1973.
- In 2006 the South Dakota legislature proposed a bill banning all abortions. Meant to challenge *Roe v. Wade*, it was voted down during the 2006 midterm elections.
- Approximately 1.3 million abortions are performed in the United States each year.
- Two percent of all women between the ages of fifteen and forty-four will seek an abortion at least once in their lifetimes.
- Doctors in forty-seven states can legally refuse to perform abortions on moral grounds.
- More than thirty states have laws making it a homicide to kill a fetus.

- Only 11 percent of Americans believe abortion should be permitted after the sixth month of pregnancy, according to a poll by ABC News.
- According to a poll taken by the Pew Research Center in July 2006:

  Sixty-six percent of Americans believe that the country needs to find a middle ground on abortion law, while only 29 percent say that there is no room for compromise.

  Fifty-five percent of Americans prefer that abortion law be decided at the federal rather than state level.

  Two-thirds of conservative Republicans say that abortion should only be available in cases of rape or incest, when the mother's life is threatened, or not at all. By contrast, three-quarters of liberal Democrats say that abortion should either be generally available or available with some limits.

According to the Alan Guttmacher Institute:
- Approximately 50 percent of all abortions performed in the United States each year are repeat abortions, compared to 12 percent in 1973.
- The rate of teenagers seeking abortions has declined in recent years. In 2000, 19 percent of women seeking abortions were teenagers, as opposed to 33 percent in 1972.
- In Mississippi, Kentucky, and the Dakotas, 98 percent of all counties have no abortion providers. In Missouri and Nebraska, 97 percent of counties have none.
- Sixty percent of women who seek an abortion are already parents.

According to the Center for Reproductive Rights:
- In thirty states, women must wait twenty-four hours after seeking an abortion before they can have the procedure.
- Seven states do not provide abortions for women with Medicaid, the federal health insurance for the poor. Three states voluntarily provide abortions for women on Medicaid, while thirteen states have been ordered to do so by the courts.

Abortion Around the World

- Approximately 20 million women worldwide have unsafe abortions each year, and seventy thousand die as a result, according to the World Health Organization.
- Twenty-six percent of the world's population lives in countries where abortion is prohibited, according to the Center for Reproductive Rights.
- Latin America has the world's strictest laws on abortion. It also has the world's highest abortion rate: approximately one per woman in her lifetime, according to the *New York Times.*
- In 2006 the country of Nicaragua passed a law banning all abortions, including cases of rape and incest and cases in which the mother's life is threatened. The country of El Salvador has had such a law since 1998.

Glossary

abortifacient: Most often, a drug or other chemical substance that causes abortion in a pregnant woman.

***Ayotte v. Planned Parenthood of Northern New England*:** The January 2006 U.S. Supreme Court decision stating that abortion laws must protect pregnant women's health and safety. The case was spurred by the passage of a New Hampshire law that required doctors to notify a pregnant teenager's parents before performing an abortion, with no provision for the health of the teenager.

Down syndrome: A genetic disorder characterized by mild to moderate mental retardation, as well as various physical traits such as weak muscles and short stature.

embryo: From implantation in the uterus until the eighth week of development, the product of conception.

emergency contraception: A certain type of drug with a high dose of hormones that can be taken after unprotected sex to prevent pregnancy. Also called the morning-after pill.

eugenics: Attempting to control the makeup of the human race by selectively choosing certain qualities in fetuses, children, or parents.

fetus: From the eighth week of conception until the moment of birth, the unborn baby contained in the pregnant woman's uterus.

***Planned Parenthood v. Casey*:** The 1992 U.S. Supreme Court decision upholding *Roe v. Wade* while giving states the authority to place some limits on abortions.

pro-choice: The term used by abortion supporters to describe themselves and their views.

pro-life: The term used by abortion opponents to describe themselves and their views.

Roe v. Wade: The 1973 U.S. Supreme Court decision that legalized abortion in the United States. *Roe v. Wade* determined that a woman had a constitutional right to an abortion until a certain point in the pregnancy, based on privacy rights.

vacuum aspiration: The most common abortion method. Used early in the pregnancy, the uterus is emptied with a suction device. Also called a D&C, dilation and suction curettage.

Organizations to Contact

Alan Guttmacher Institute
120 Wall St.
New York, NY 10005
(212) 248-1111
fax: (212) 248-1951
e-mail: info@guttmacher.org
Web site: www.alanguttmacher.org

The institute works to protect and expand the reproductive choices of all women and men. It strives to ensure people's access to the information and services they need to exercise their rights and responsibilities concerning sexual activity, reproduction, and family planning. Among the institute's publications are "Abortion and Mental Health: Myths and Realities," and "Minors and the Right to Consent to Health Care."

Center for Bioethics and Human Dignity
2065 Half Day Rd.
Bannockburn, IL 60015
(847) 317-8180
fax: (847) 317-8101
e-mail: info@cbhd.org
Web site: www.cbhd.org

The Center for Bioethics and Human Dignity is a nonprofit organization that applies a Christian perspective to issues of science, biomedicine, and biotechnology. The center uses biblical values in examining issues of cloning, stem cell research, and abortion, among others. The organization produces many articles and audiobooks, including "Abortion Debate: Back to the Future," and "Abortion and Women: The Untold Story."

Center for Reproductive Rights
120 Wall St.
New York, NY 10005
(917) 637-3600
fax: (917) 637-3666
e-mail: info@reprorights.org
Web site: www.crlp.org

The mission of the Center for Reproductive Rights is to protect women's right to health care, with a focus on family planning and contraception. The organization also works to ensure that women around the world have access to safe abortions, as well as in the United States. The center monitors global abortion laws and lobbies governments to expand abortion rights. The group publishes an extensive list of articles and policy papers such as "Breaking the Silence: The Global Gag Rule's Impact on Unsafe Abortion," as well as instructional material for activists, such as "From Rights to Reality: How to Advocate for Women's Reproductive Rights Worldwide."

Concerned Women for America (CWA)
1015 Fifteenth St. NW, Suite 1100
Washington, DC 20005
(202) 488-7000
fax: (202) 488-0806
Web site: www.cwfa.org

CWA's purpose is to preserve, protect, and promote traditional Judeo-Christian values through education, legislative action, and other activities. It is concerned with creating an environment that is conducive to building strong families and raising healthy children. CWA publishes the monthly *Family Voice*, which periodically addresses issues such as abortion and birth control.

Family Research Council (FRC)
801 G St. NW
Washington, DC 20001
(202) 393-2100
fax: (202) 393-2134
Web site: www.frc.org

The FRC seeks to promote and protect the interests of the traditional family. It focuses on issues such as parental autonomy and responsibility, community support for single parents, and abortion. Among the council's numerous publications are the booklets *Partial-Birth Abortion on Trial* and *Building a Culture of Life Thirty Years After* Roe.

Feminists for Life of America
PO Box 20685
Alexandria, VA 22320
(703) 836-3354
e-mail: info@feministsforlife.org
Web site: www.feministsforlife.org

Feminists for Life is an advocacy group that believes that abortion is harmful to women and women's rights. The group is dedicated to spreading this viewpoint through their publications and Web site and media campaigns. Feminists for Life publishes a quarterly magazine, *American Feminist*.

Focus on the Family
8605 Explorer Dr.
Colorado Springs, CO 80920
(719) 531-3400
fax: (719) 531-3424
Web site: www.focusonthefamily.org

Focus on the Family is a Christian organization dedicated to preserving and strengthening the traditional family. It believes that the breakdown of the traditional family is in part linked to increases in teen pregnancy and abortion, and so it conducts research on the ethics of condom use and the effectiveness of safe-sex education programs in schools. The organization publishes a monthly magazine, *Focus*.

The Heritage Foundation
214 Massachusetts Ave. NE
Washington, DC 20002

(202) 546-4400
fax: (202) 546-8328
e-mail: info@heritage.org
Web site: www.heritage.org

The Heritage Foundation is a public policy research institute that supports the ideas of limited government and the free-market system. It promotes the view that the welfare system has contributed to the problems of illegitimacy and teenage pregnancy. The foundation promotes abstinence over contraception and abortion. Among the foundation's numerous publications is its Backgrounder series, which includes "Liberal Welfare Programs: What the Data Show on Programs for Teenage Mothers" and the paper "Rising Illegitimacy: America's Social Catastrophe."

National Abortion and Reproductive Rights Action League (NARAL Pro-Choice America)
1156 Fifteenth St. NW, Suite 700
Washington, DC 20005
(202) 973-3000
fax: (202) 973-3096
Web site: www.prochoiceamerica.org

The goal of NARAL, which has groups in more than forty states, is to develop and sustain a pro-choice political constituency in order to maintain the right of all women to legal abortion. The league briefs members of Congress and testifies at hearings on abortion and related issues. It publishes the quarterly *NARAL Newsletter*.

National Abortion Federation (NAF)
1755 Massachusetts Ave. NW, Suite 600
Washington, DC 20036
(202) 667-5881
fax: (202) 667-5890
e-mail: naf@prochoice.org
Web site: www.prochoice.org

The NAF is the professional association for doctors who perform abortions in the United States. The association provides resources, training, and support for its members as well as working to promote safe, legal, and accessible abortions. The NAF publishes numerous professional papers and newsletters such as *Providing Early Options* and *Clinicians for Choice.*

National Organization for Women (NOW)
1100 H St. NW, 3rd Fl.
Washington, DC 20005
(202) 628-8669
fax: (202) 785-8576
Web site: www.now.org

The National Organization for Women is the largest feminist activist organization in the United States. A nonprofit organization, NOW's mission is to promote equal rights and justice for women on a variety of social issues, including birth control and abortion. The *NOW Times* is the organization's quarterly newsletter.

National Right to Life Committee (NRLC)
512 Tenth St. NW
Washington, DC 20004
(202) 626-8800
e-mail: nrlc@nrlc.org
Web site: www.nrlc.org

The NRLC is one of the largest pro-life organizations in the United States. The committee opposes legalized abortion and promotes alternatives such as adoption through lobbying, media campaigns, and grassroots advocacy. The NRLC publishes an online newsletter, the *National Right to Life News.*

Planned Parenthood Federation of America
434 W. Thirty-third St.
New York, NY 10001
(212) 541-7800
fax: (212) 245-1845
e-mail: communications@ppfa.org
Web site: www.plannedparenthood.org

Planned Parenthood is a national organization that supports people's right to make their own reproductive decisions without governmental interference. It provides contraceptive counseling and abortions at its many clinics throughout the United States. Planned Parenthood publishes kits for parents, educators, and medical professionals. It also maintains the Web site Teenwire.com, which provides reproductive health information for adolescents.

Pro-Choice Action Network
1755 Robson St., Suite 512
Vancouver, BC, Canada V6G 3B7
(604) 736-2800
e-mail: info@prochoiceactionnetwork-canada.org
Web site: www.prochoiceactionnetwork-canada.org

This Canadian nonprofit organization seeks to protect and expand abortion rights through government lobbying, as well as grassroots campaigns, marches, and rallies. The network forms partnerships with other abortion rights groups and providers to provide mutual support. The Pro-Choice Action Network publishes a quarterly newsletter, *Pro-Choice Press*.

Pro-Life Action League
6160 N. Cicero Ave., Suite 600
Chicago, IL 60646
(312) 777-2900
fax (312) 777-3061
e-mail: info@prolifeaction.org
Web site: www.prolifeaction.org

The Pro-Life Action League is an activist group that works to end legal abortion. The league organizes demonstrations at abortion clinics, as well as other agencies that provide abortion services or advice. The group publishes a pro-life activist manual titled *Closed: 99 Ways to Stop Abortion*, as well as an online newspaper, *Current Action News*.

Sexuality Information and Education Council of the United States (SIECUS)
130 W. Forty-second St., Suite 350
New York, NY 10036
(212) 819-9770
fax: (212) 819-9776
e-mail: siecus@siecus.org
Web site: www.siecus.org

SIECUS develops, collects, and disseminates information on human sexuality. It promotes comprehensive education about sexuality and advocates the right of individuals to make responsible sexual choices. In addition to providing guidelines for sexuality education for kindergarten through twelfth grades, SIECUS publishes numerous reports, booklets, magazines, and newsletters in both English and Spanish.

For Further Reading

Books

Randy Alcorn, *Why Pro-Life? Caring for the Unborn and Their Mothers*. Sisters, OR: Multnomah, 2004. This book, written by a minister, makes the case against abortion from a Christian perspective.

Erika Bachiochi, *The Cost of "Choice": Women Evaluate the Impact of Abortion*. New York: Encounter, 2007. A book offering a pro-life view of abortion.

Robert M. Baird and Stuart E. Rosenbaum, *The Ethics of Abortion: Pro-Life vs. Pro-Choice*. Amherst, NY: Prometheus, 2001. The authors of this young adult book aim to present a balanced view of different arguments on abortion.

Jack M. Balkin, *What* Roe v. Wade *Should Have Said: The Nation's Top Legal Experts Rewrite America's Most Controversial Decision*. New York: New York University Press, 2005. This anthology presents a collection of essays discussing the pros and cons of the *Roe v. Wade* Supreme Court opinion.

Andrea Bonavoglia, *The Choices We Made: Twenty-five Women and Men Speak Out About Abortion*. New York: Four Walls Eight Windows, 2001. This book contains interviews with well-known people about their experiences with abortion.

Gene Burns, *The Moral Veto: Framing Contraception, Abortion, and Cultural Pluralism in the United States*. New York: Cambridge University Press, 2005. This book presents the history of moral controversies in the United States, including that of abortion.

Lydia A. Clarke, *Can't Keep Silent: A Woman's 22-Year Journey of Post-abortion Healing*. Mustang, OK: Tate, 2006. An autobiographical account of the author's experience with abortion.

J. Shoshanna Ehrlich, *Who Decides? The Abortion Rights of Teens*. Westport, CT: Praeger, 2006. A legal-education professor discusses the issue of parental and judicial involvement in teen abortion.

Anibel Faundes and Jose Barzelatto, *The Human Drama of Abortion: A Global Search for Consensus*. Nashville, TN: Vanderbilt University Press, 2006. Two doctors present personal experiences of abortion from women around the world and examine various countries' abortion policies.

Gloria Feldt, *Behind Every Choice Is a Story*. Denton: University of North Texas Press, 2003. The author presents first-person stories of women who have made the decision to have an abortion.

Anne Hendershott, *The Politics of Abortion*. New York: Encounter, 2006. The author examines important legislation, court cases, and social issues relating to the abortion debate in the United States.

Krista Jacob, *Abortion Under Attack: Women on the Challenges Facing Choice*. Emeryville, CA: Seal, 2006. This anthology presents essays by prominent feminists and activists discussing the challenges of preserving abortion rights.

Vasu Murti, *The Liberal Case Against Abortion*. R.A.G.E. Media, 2006. A self-identified liberal activist argues against abortion using liberal philosophy.

Cristina Page, *How the Pro-Choice Movement Saved America*. Cambridge, MA: Basic, 2006. The author argues that the pro-life movement is misogynistic and dangerous to women's health.

Ramesh Ponnuru, *The Party of Death: The Democrats, the Media, the Courts, and the Disregard for Human Life*. Washington, DC: Regnery, 2006. A conservative author argues that the Democratic Party has little regard for human life, including that of fetuses.

John M. Riddle, *Contraception and Abortion from the Ancient World to the Renaissance*. Cambridge, MA: Harvard University Press, 1994. This book presents the history of birth control.

William Saletan, *Bearing Right: How Conservatives Won the Abortion War*. Berkeley and Los Angeles: University of California Press, 2004. This book discusses abortion from a political point of view. The author argues that the pro-life movement has been more successful than the pro-choice movement.

Alexander Sanger, *Beyond Choice: Reproductive Freedom in the 21st Century*. New York: PublicAffairs, 2004. The author argues that the pro-choice movement is ineffective in promoting abortion rights and suggests changes.

Johanna Schoen, *Choice and Coercion: Birth Control, Sterilization, and Abortion in Public Health and Welfare.* Chapel Hill: University of North Carolina Press, 2005. This scholarly book discusses government policies on reproduction as they relate to the poor and underprivileged.

Rickie Solinger, *Abortion Wars: A Half Century of Struggle, 1950–2000.* Berkeley and Los Angeles: University of California Press, 1998. This book offers a pro-choice collection of historical essays on abortion.

Periodicals

Daniel Allot, "The Abortion Effect," *American Spectator*, January 24, 2006.

America, "The Abortion Debate Today," February 16, 2004.

Justine Andronici, "Reproductive Rights on Trial—Again," *Ms.*, Winter 2006.

Doug Bandow, "Freedom to Choose to Refuse," *American Spectator*, June 9, 2005.

Patricia E. Bauer, "The Abortion Debate No One Wants to Have," *Washington Post*, October 18, 2005.

David Brooks, "*Roe*'s Birth, and Death," *New York Times*, April 21, 2005.

Lorie Chaiten, "Leave Pregnant Women to Decide Their Own Morals," *Chicago Sun-Times*, January 25, 2005.

Dalton Conley, "A Man's Right to Choose," *New York Times*, December 1, 2005.

Mark H. Creech, "Welcoming Life with Cheers," *Christian Post*, November 12, 2004.

Jennifer Dalve, "Is New Hampshire's Parental Abortion Act Constitutional?" *Supreme Court Debates*, January 2006.

Meghan Daum, "Crowding Out a Right to Choose," *Los Angeles Times*, March 4, 2006.

Economist, "A Life and Choice Matter," May 1, 2004.

Barbara Ehrenreich, "Owning Up to Abortion," *New York Times*, July 22, 2004.

Clarke D. Forsythe, "Supreme Opportunity," *National Review*, November 30, 2005.

Garance Franke-Ruta, "Liberal Concerns About Abortion," *New Republic*, November 28, 2005.

Ellen Goodman, "Whose Conscience Rules?" *Boston Globe*, April 10, 2005.

Carole Joffe, "Reproductive Regression," *TomPaine.com*, January 23, 2006.

Antony Barone Kolenc, "Easing Abortion's Pain," *America*, September 26, 2005.

Anne Lamott, "The Rights of the Born," *Los Angeles Times*, February 10, 2006.

Dahlia Lithwick, "Are Judges the New Doctors?" *Slate*, August 12, 2005.

Kathryn Jean Lopez, "We Deserve Better than *Roe*," *National Review*, April 5, 2006.

Rich Lowry, "Bundle of Linguistic Confusion," *National Review Online*, December 21, 2004. www.nationalreview.com.

Kate Michelman, "Pro-Family, Pro-Choice, Pro-Women," *TomPaine.com*, March 6, 2006.

National Catholic Reporter, "A New Approach to Reducing Abortions," September 24, 2004.

George Neumayr, "One of America's Cures for Disability Is Death," *American Spectator*, June 2005.

Daniel Oliver, "Deciding Abortion," *National Review*, May 9, 2005.

Ted Olsen, "The Art of Abortion Politics," *Christianity Today*, March 2006.

Lynn M. Paltrow, "The Pregnancy Police," *Alternet.org*, June 7, 2006.

Ramesh Ponnuru, "Partial Truth," *National Review*, May 1, 2006.

William Saletan, "The Issue That Never Went Away," *New York Times*, April 25, 2004.

Reina Schiffrin and Joann D. Smith, "Don't Let Abortion Foes Chip Away at *Roe*," *Newsday*, December 1, 2005.

Stuart Taylor Jr., "Opening Argument," *National Journal*, December 3, 2005.

Rebecca Traister, "*Roe* for Men?" *Salon.com*, March 13, 2006.

Gene Edward Veith, "Hearts of Stone," *World Magazine*, August 7, 2004.

C. Joshua Villines, "Lacking Basis, Christians Fight Abortion," *Atlanta Journal-Constitution*, March 20, 2006.

George F. Will, "Eugenics by Abortion," *Washington Post*, April 14, 2005.

Lynda Zielinski, "Jane Doe's Choice," *Ms.*, Winter 2006.

Web Sites

Human Life International (www.hli.org). This organization bills itself as "pro-life missionaries to the world." The Catholic-oriented group has extensive resources devoted to fighting abortion on its Web site.

Pro-Choice Public Education Project (www.protectchoice.org). This abortion-rights organization is geared toward providing young women and teenagers with information about abortion and abortion policy. The group holds rallies and demonstrations in support of legal abortion and provides an online chat forum on its Web site.

Pro-Choice Talk Forum (www.prochoicetalk.com). This public debate forum offers a place for abortion-rights supporters to share information, as well as a space in which to engage and debate abortion opponents who join the online discussion.

Second Look Project (www.secondlookproject.org). Second Look is a pro-life media campaign that seeks to dissuade women from abortion by offering them information about their developing babies. The Web site offers links to Second Look's radio and print advertisements.

Teen Wire (www.teenwire.com). A sexual health Web site specifically for teens, run by Planned Parenthood of America. Includes articles written by teens about sex, answers to commonly asked questions, and information on pregnancy and sexually transmitted diseases.

Index

Supreme Court
on assisted suicide, 49
on women's health exception,
84
See also specific cases

T
Terry, Randall, 53
TRAP laws, 41

U
Ultrasound technology, 23
pro-choice argument and, 25

Unborn Victims of Violence Act
(2005), 25, 42
U.S. Constitution, Fourteen
Amendment, 35

W
Wade, Roe v. See Roe v. Wade
White, Byron, 38
Women's rights
pro-choice view associated
with, 8–9
rights of fetus conflict with,
13–14

Picture Credits

Cover photo: Photos.com
Maury Aaseng, 15, 20, 24, 36, 40, 48, 52, 58, 62, 69, 74, 81, 85, 93
© ANSA/ANSA/Corbis, 57
AP Images, 11, 13, 19, 23, 31, 34, 37, 41, 42, 44, 46, 67, 73, 77, 86, 91
BananaStock/JupiterImages Unlimited, 8
© David S. Holloway/Getty Images, 11